"I didn't cause the accident, so I'm not giving you a dime, and that's that!" Declan crossed his arms and jutted his jaw.

"Fine! I'll have my dad call yours. Then we'll see who'll pay for the repairs. One thing's for certain. I'm not dipping into *my* savings to pay for it. Every penny I have is for the class ski trip this winter. There's no way I'm passing up on that!" Greg shot back.

"Oh, dear. It's getting ugly between those two." Luana hated hearing the boys fight. "Perhaps we should see if we can help."

Phoebe gawked at her. "Help? How?"

Luana stared into space, twisting a long dark braid around her fingers—a habit she had whenever she was anxious, upset, or preoccupied. She bolted upright after a few moments; her entire face lit up.

"Oh, no." Phoebe groaned. "I know that look. It usually means work—for me!"

Luana giggled. "Come on, Pheebs. I just thought we should offer to hear the boys' case in the Kids' Court. What do you think?"

Phoebe's eyes shone. "That's a great idea, Lu!"

Join the **KIDS' COURT** & solve these other mysteries

#1 The Doll Dilemma

#2 The Go-KartAstrophe

#3 The Goody Bag Goner

#4 The Cookie Caper

A KIDS' COURT WHODUNIT
THE GO-KARTASTROPHE
BY CARON PESCATORE

Copyright © 2017, 2022 by Caron Pescatore.

All rights reserved. No part of this publication may be reproduced, distributed, or transmitted in any form or by any means, including photocopying, recording, or other electronic or mechanical methods, without the prior written permission of the publisher, except in the case of brief quotations embodied in critical reviews and certain other noncommercial uses permitted by copyright law.

Cover Design by Best Page Forward
https://www.bestpageforward.net/

Edited by Kate Angelella
https://www.angelellaeditorial.com/

ISBN-13: 978-0997587999

Library of Congress Control Number: 2022902499

LCCN Imprint Name: Caron Pescatore, Fort Lauderdale

IMPRINT: PESKY BOOKS 4KIDZ

An Imprint of Caron Pescatore, Fort Lauderdale, FL

All characters and storylines are the author's property, and I appreciate your support and respect. The characters and events portrayed in this book are fictitious. Any similarities to actual persons, living or dead, are coincidental and not intended by the author.

Published 2022
First published February 2017
Second edition published February 2022

Printed in the United States of America

Kids' Court Staff

Luana
Defense Lawyer

Lindsey
Court Reporter

Jake
Court Bailiff

Heather
Judge

Mary Beth
Plaintiff's Lawyer

Ashley
Private Investigator

Phoebe
Private Investigator

*For my husband,
who encouraged me every step of the way;
and for my children,
the best creative team a writer could ask for!*

Table of Contents

Dollars and Sense 1

Meet the Players 13

Court is in Session 27

Tireless Testimony 41

Hard as Nails 51

A Colorful Witness 63

A Nervous Wreck 75

Trials and Trails 87

Dance of Truth 99

All's Well That Ends Well 109

Trick... or Cheat? 125

Glossary 137

CHAPTER 1

Dollars and Sense

"HOW MANY TIMES do I have to tell you?" Declan Mathias shouted. *"It wasn't my fault!"*

"So what are you saying, Dec? The kart ran into the tree by itself?" Greg Foster scoffed.

"Something was wrong with the go-kart," said Declan. "I couldn't turn the wheel."

"Oh, please," said Greg. "I'd say the problem was you turned the wheel too hard. I saw you wrench it. That's what caused the kart to spin out of control. There was absolutely nothing wrong with it before that. But now it's in pieces, thanks to you."

Declan rolled his eyes. Greg was his best friend, but his tendency to exaggerate—which he often did—was beyond annoying. This was especially true when Greg told stories about his various athletic achievements. The go-kart was most definitely *not* "in pieces."

CARON PESCATORE

Next door, eleven-year-old Luana Porcello sighed. "Those two have been arguing nonstop ever since Declan crashed Greg's go-kart two days ago," she said to her best friend, Phoebe Chen. The two girls were lying out by the pool in Luana's backyard.

After they'd spent the morning helping Luana's mom clean the attic, the girls had planned to have a relaxing afternoon. Unfortunately, the ongoing argument next door shattered their peace.

"What's the big deal, anyway?" said Phoebe. "Why don't they just fix it? I mean, they're the ones who built the stupid thing in the first place." She rolled her eyes as she sat up and gathered her midnight-black hair into a ponytail, securing it on top of her head with a dark-blue scrunchy she slid from her right wrist.

Luana chuckled, the dimples in her cheeks popping. "I don't think it's that simple, Pheebs. It sounds like the go-kart needs major repairs, and Greg doesn't have the money to fix it."

They could hear the boys still going at it in the background.

"You messed up and wrecked my kart," said Greg. "Now, you need to pay to fix it."

"I don't care what you say," said Declan. "The go-kart wasn't working right. It kept going straight, even though I spun the steering wheel. That's why it ran into the tree. I'll go fifty-fifty with you on the repairs, but that's it. And you're lucky I'm willing to do that much. You gave me a defective go-kart to drive. I could have been seriously hurt if I hadn't jumped out before it crashed."

"You've got some nerve!" Greg bellowed. "My go-kart is not 'defective.' You're so overly dramatic. First, you beg me to let you drive the kart, then you smash it to smithereens, and now you're whining like a baby about injuries you don't have." He ticked off Declan's offenses on his fingers as he listed each one.

"I did not beg you to drive the go-kart, and I'm not a baby! And who are *you* to call *me* overly dramatic?" Declan said. "You're the one who's blowing the damage to the kart out of proportion. It's not 'smashed to smithereens'—not even close. All it has is a bent frame and a broken steering column. You should be thanking me. If I hadn't slowed down before it hit that tree, the cart would really be in pieces." He shook his head. "You know what? Forget it. I didn't cause the accident, so I'm not giving you a dime. And that's that!" He crossed his arms and jutted his jaw.

"Fine! I'll have my dad call yours. Then we'll see who'll pay for the repairs. One thing's for certain. I'm not dipping into *my* savings to pay for it. Every penny I have is for the class ski trip this winter. There's no way I'm passing up on that!" The annual ski trip was the highlight of the eighth-grade school year, and both boys were eagerly looking forward to the three-day excursion.

"Oh, dear. It's getting ugly between those two." Luana's mouth turned down at the corners. She hated hearing the boys fight. They were best friends and had been inseparable since Declan moved into the neighborhood six years ago. "Perhaps we should see if we can help."

Phoebe gawked at her. "Help? How?"

Luana stared into space, twisting a long dark braid around her fingers—a habit she had whenever she was anxious, upset, or preoccupied. She bolted upright after a few moments; her entire face lit up.

"Oh, no." Phoebe groaned. "I know that look. It usually means work—for me!"

Luana giggled. "Come on, Pheebs. I just thought we should offer to hear the boys' case in the Kids' Court. What do you think?"

Phoebe's eyes shone. "That's a great idea, Lu!" She sprang from her lounge chair and marched across the yard.

"Hey, where are you going?" Luana called after her.

"To talk to the boys," Phoebe yelled over her shoulder. "There's no time like the present—the sooner they go to court, the sooner we'll get our peace back!"

It was just like Phoebe to charge ahead without thinking. Her impetuous nature had gotten her into trouble more than a time or two.

But Luana had to admit her friend had a point. *The sooner we help the boys settle their argument, the sooner we can get back to relaxing,* she thought. Chuckling to herself, Luana headed next door, following at a slower pace. As she neared the Fosters' garage, she could hear Phoebe's voice.

"You two need to quit arguing! I can't hear myself think over all the bickering."

"We aren't bickering," Greg retorted. "We're having a serious discussion. But I wouldn't expect a little kid to understand the difference."

"Who are you calling a little kid? I'm not the one whining over a toy."

"My go-kart is not a toy!" said Greg, sounding outraged. "It's a motorized veh—"

"Yeah, yeah, yeah! Whatever. I don't care if it's a

Lamborghini made of pure gold. I want you two to keep it down so I can get some peace."

"Um, Pheebs." Luana stood by the open garage door, peeking in. "We came over here to help . . . remember?"

"Help?" said Declan. "How can you help?"

"We overheard your–er–conversation," said Luana, advancing into the garage.

"Yeah. No doubt the entire neighborhood heard you." Phoebe's upper lip curled as she eyed the two boys.

"I thought perhaps you would consider taking your case to court." Luana bit the inside of her cheek and crossed the fingers of one hand behind her back.

"Court?" Greg knitted his brows. "I'd love to take

THE GO-KARTASTROPHE

Declan to court. Someone needs to make him pay for the damage to my go-kart. But what court would take my case?"

"A few of us started the Kids' Court," said Luana.

"I told you about it, remember?" said Declan. "I testified in Jenny Corbett's case against her twin, Jimmy."

"Oh yeah." Greg pinched his bottom lip. "You know, going to court isn't a bad idea," he said after a while. "But this is no game. It's serious business. How can I trust a court run by a bunch of little kids?" He cocked his head and looked down at the two girls as though he were an adult talking to slow-witted children.

Phoebe bristled, her eyes shooting daggers at Greg. "Stop calling us little kids! For your information, Luana did an amazing job defending Jimmy against his sister's claim that he destroyed her doll!"

Luana's dusky-brown cheeks reddened. "It was more of a team effort. The Kids' Court is the real thing. It's a court like any other, except we handle cases involving disagreements between kids, not grown-ups. We have a judge, a bailiff, and a court reporter. And, of course, we have attorneys to represent the plaintiff and the defendant."

"Say what?" Greg's eyes widened. "I didn't get half of what you just said."

Luana scrunched up her face. "Sorry. I hear so much legal talk from my parents that I forget not everyone understands the jargon. I assume you know what a judge is—most people do. As for the rest, it's pretty simple. A court reporter is like a personal assistant, and it's her job to keep a record of each case by typing everything said in court. A bailiff is a sheriff's deputy who protects the judge and makes sure everyone follows the court's rules."

Greg and Declan nodded in understanding.

"The plaintiff and defendant are the parties to the case," Luana continued. "The plaintiff files a complaint with the court, accusing the defendant of wrongdoing. As the accuser, it's the plaintiff's job to prove the defendant's guilt to the court."

"It sounds like when I tell Mom Matty did something wrong; I have to convince her he did it. She's always saying, 'Where is the proof, Greg? You've gotta have some proof.'" He spoke in a high-pitched tone, attempting to mimic his mother's voice.

Luana giggled. "It's exactly like that."

"OK, that sounds good. What about lawyers and stuff?" asked Greg.

"We have lawyers—two of them. The defendant and the plaintiff each get one to speak for them in court." Luana shrugged. "That's about it in a nutshell. Do you guys have questions?"

"*Ahem.*" Phoebe raised her hand in the air. "I have a question."

A slight frown marred Luana's features. "What is it, Pheebs?"

Phoebe jutted her right hip and folded her arms across her chest, glaring at Luana in mock anger. "Aren't you forgetting something?"

Luana's frown deepened. "I don't think—Oh!" She gasped and covered her mouth with both hands. "I'm sorry, Pheebs." She smacked her forehead with a palm. "I forgot," she said to the boys. "We also have private investigators. One for the plaintiff and one for the defendant."

Greg's mouth twitched. "I assume Little Bit here is one of the private investigators?" He jerked a thumb toward Phoebe.

"Who are you calling 'Little Bit'?" Phoebe growled. Although she was tiny, Phoebe's personality was larger than life, and she hated anyone drawing attention to her small size.

"Phoebe is quite the detective," said Luana, defending her friend. She nibbled on her lower lip and regarded the boys with solemn amber eyes. "So, what do you say? Do you want to take your case to the Kids' Court?"

Noticing their hesitation, she added, "It could help you figure out the cause of the accident. Daddy says there's no better way to get to the truth than by having a trial. That way, a neutral person listens to all the evidence and decides what really happened." Luana's father was a senior lawyer with the district attorney's office, prosecuting people accused of committing crimes.

"I already know what happened," said Greg. "I just want Declan to pay to fix the go-kart when the court finds him guilty."

"The court won't find me guilty because I'm not!" Declan shot back.

"We'll see," said Greg. "All I'm saying is that you need to pay up if or *when* you're found guilty."

Declan glowered at Greg.

"That's one of our court's conditions," said Luana. "You must promise to accept the verdict."

"What do you mean?" asked Declan.

"She means that you and he"—Phoebe jerked her head toward Greg—"must agree to accept the judge's decision, even if she decides against you."

"That's how it is in real courts, too," said Luana.

THE GO-KARTASTROPHE

"Except, in a real court, the judge has ways to enforce her orders. She can put you in jail or order you to pay a fine, to name a couple. Our judge can't make people follow her orders; we have to rely on the honor system. So everyone who comes to the Kids' Court must promise to follow the judge's orders and accept her verdict. Otherwise, it would be a waste of time to have a trial."

"Yeah," said Phoebe. "Think about it. If we had your trial and the judge ruled Declan caused the accident, but he refused to pay to fix the go-kart, we would have wasted all that time."

"I see your point." Declan ran a hand over his dark afro.

"And that's why we ask you each to make a promise," said Luana. "Declan, you must promise to pay for the repairs if the judge finds you guilty. And Greg, you must promise to accept the court's verdict as final even if the judge says Declan is not guilty. Can you both do that?"

Declan crossed his arms and nodded. "Yeah, I can," he said readily.

Greg hesitated, shoved his hands into his jeans pockets, and hunched his shoulders. "Me too."

Luana narrowed her eyes. "Are you sure, Greg?"

His eyes slid away from hers. "Yeah, I'm sure."

She studied him for a moment, then shrugged. "OK. Then let's plan to meet after lunch. Come in through the basement door on the other side of my house. That's the courtroom. I'll call the others to let them know we have a case!"

CHAPTER 2

Meet the Players

MARY BETH STOVER bounced into the courtroom, accompanied by her younger sister, Ashley. "This is so exciting. I can't believe we have *another* case." Her deep-blue eyes sparkled.

"We sure do," said Phoebe. "We forced the two buffoons to bring their case to court. They were driving me nuts!"

"Which two buffoons?" Ashley perched on the edge of a chair at the defense table, where Phoebe sat with Luana, Jake, and Lindsey.

"Declan Mathias and Greg Foster." Phoebe scowled.

"Hey, those are my friends you're talking about! They're not buffoons." As usual, strands of Jake Crandall's reddish-blond hair were sticking out in every direction. He was the court's bailiff, a position he enthusiastically embraced when they first started the Kids' Court.

"Well, they sure have been acting like buffoons," said Phoebe. "It's been nonstop bickering between those two ever since they crashed Greg's go-kart. I couldn't stand it anymore!"

"They have been rather loud," said Lindsey Harrison in her soft voice. At ten, she was a year younger than the rest of the group, except Ashley, who was nine. "I can hear them from my yard, and I live two houses away on the opposite side of the street!" When she noticed the other children staring at her, she blushed and ducked her head, wondering what had possessed her to speak up.

"You see?" said Phoebe. "Even Lindsey can hear them!"

"You just don't get it." Jake got to his feet and towered over Phoebe. His enormous size, loud voice, and forceful manner of speaking made him intimidating to kids who didn't know him. But his friends knew that beneath his gruff exterior was a sweet, fiercely loyal boy.

"What's there to get?" asked Phoebe. "It's a stupid go-kart."

"First, the go-kart isn't stupid. But I wouldn't

THE GO-KARTASTROPHE

expect a *girl* to understand that." He placed his hands on the table and leaned toward Phoebe, giving her a withering look.

Phoebe put her thumbs in her ears and twiddled her fingers back and forth as she stuck her tongue out at Jake.

He rolled his eyes. "And second, because of the crash, Greg's probably going to miss the Race-A-Thon."

"I don't see why." Ashley wrapped a blond curl around her finger. "The races don't start for another two weeks." Although the sisters looked alike, their personalities were as different as night and day. Because while Ashley was level-headed and resolute, Mary Beth was a total scatterbrain, and her mindset was like a reed blowing in the wind—first going one way and then the other.

"Yeah, but the entry period starts on Wednesday, and it's only three days long," said Jake. "If you miss it, you miss it. Today's Saturday. If Greg doesn't get the money he needs to repair the go-kart soon, he'll miss the window."

"Why can't he enter the race, then fix the go-kart?" asked Mary Beth. "As Ashley said, he has two weeks until the races begin."

"Because, duh, when you apply for the entry, they inspect your vehicle, *and* you have to do a practice race to prove you're a skillful driver," said Jake. "They don't just let anyone enter."

"He has to do a practice run when he enters?" Mary Beth wrinkled her nose.

"Didn't I just say that?" Jake huffed. "And if his kart doesn't pass inspection, he can forget it. They have hundreds of people trying to enter the races during those three days, maybe even thousands. They don't give do-overs. If you don't pass inspection, you're out."

"Well, I don't see why he has to do a practice run," said Mary Beth. "Why would anyone own a go thingy if they didn't know how to drive it? And why can't they extend the time for people to enter?"

THE GO-KARTASTROPHE

Jake pressed his palms against his temples. "Just because you own a *go-kart* doesn't mean you're a good enough driver to race," he retorted. "And—"

"Who cares?" Phoebe waved her hand dismissively. "The point is, I'm tired of listening to them rehash the same issue over and over without coming to any solution. It's annoying! That's why Luana suggested they take their case to the Kids' Court."

"Actually, I suggested it because they're going to ruin their friendship unless we help them figure out what caused the accident. I'd hate to see that happen." Luana was a sweet-natured girl who hated seeing anyone unhappy, especially her friends.

While the children were talking, Declan arrived. He was a broad-shouldered boy of average height with dark skin, thick black hair, and deep-set brown eyes. "Hey, guys."

"Hey, Dec Man," Jake greeted him. "I hear the Kids' Court is handling your case."

"Yeah." Declan sighed, rubbing the back of his neck. "I just want this whole mess to be over. Maybe Greg and I can move past it once we prove I didn't cause the crash."

"You're the defendant, Declan. It's not your job

to prove your innocence, remember? It's Greg's—" Luana broke off in the middle of her sentence as Greg strolled into the courtroom.

"Hi, guys." He walked up to the table where the group sat. "Did I hear my name?" Greg was tall for his age, with sandy-blond hair and light-green eyes. He and Declan were both athletic and played a variety of sports. But, while Declan had a laid-back, easygoing personality, Greg was competitive and intense.

"Hi, Greg." Luana raised a hand in greeting. "I was just explaining to Declan that since you are the plaintiff, it's your job to prove he's guilty, not his to prove he's innocent."

Greg ran a hand through his wavy hair. "How do I do that?"

"By bringing evidence to court that helps you prove Declan caused the accident."

"What kind of evidence?" asked Greg.

"Evidence can be anything, including witness testimony, documents, or anything else that helps you prove your case," said Luana. "For instance, if you had a video clip of Declan driving the go-kart, you could bring it to court because it shows how he drives."

"Witnesses are people who give information in

court, right?" asked Greg.

Luana nodded. "It's called testifying when a witness gives information in court. But just like other evidence, only witnesses who have facts important to the case may testify."

Phoebe sneered at Greg. "Yeah, that means you can't bring in a witness whose sole purpose is to say what a great ballplayer you are because that has nothing to do with whether Declan caused the accident."

"So, you think I'm a good ballplayer, huh? I didn't know you cared, Little Bit." Greg waggled his eyebrows at her.

Phoebe glowered at him. "Stop calling me that! And for the record, I *don't* care!"

Luana shook her head at the pair's antics. "As I was saying, only witnesses who have information about the case may testify. And Phoebe's right. Your ball-playing skills are not important to the issue. Also, you must prove your case by a 'preponderance of the evidence.' That means you must have enough evidence to prove Declan is more likely guilty than innocent. Think of it as a fifty-one, forty-nine percent split."

"A fifty-one, forty-nine percent split?" Declan furrowed his brow.

"The evidence must show that it's fifty-one percent likely you're guilty," Ashley explained.

Declan's frown deepened. "But what about 'beyond a reasonable doubt'? I hear that phrase all the time on TV."

"That's for criminal cases, where a person charged with a crime could go to jail if the court finds them guilty," said Luana. "The standard of proof for those cases is much higher. The Kids' Court is civil, where people usually sue each other for money."

"What about a jury?" asked Greg. "Isn't that who decides if someone's guilty or not?"

"We need six people for a jury in civil court," said Phoebe. "Between summer camps and family vacations, there aren't enough kids around. Unless you want a jury of little children deciding your fate." She leaned back in her chair and folded her arms, smirking at Greg.

He shrugged. "I'm already letting a bunch of little children handle my case, so . . ." Allowing his voice to trail off, Greg gave Phoebe a smug look.

She bolted upright. "Who are you calling little—"

"Enough, you two!" Luana lowered her head and pinched the bridge of her nose. "We're getting off track. Greg, we'll have a bench trial. That's where a judge decides instead of a jury. That sometimes happens in real courts, too." She regarded the two boys. "Any questions?"

Declan shook his head. "Nah. I got it."

"Me, too," said Greg.

"OK, good. We'll get started as soon as Heather arrives," said Luana.

"Heather isn't coming," said Jake.

"What!" said Phoebe. "What do you mean she's not coming?"

"She said we're to let her know when we have everything figured out," said Jake. "She said we don't need the judge until the case is ready for court, and she has 'more important' things to do." He made the quotes gesture with his fingers as he repeated his sister's words and rolled his eyes. "She was giving herself a pedicure when I left the house. And let me tell you, those hooves of hers need a lot of work, so it's just as well she didn't come."

Ashley and Lindsey giggled.

"I see." Luana chewed on her lower lip. It was just as well. Having another moody teen on her hands would only have made things more difficult. Greg and Declan were bad enough. Although Declan wasn't bad at all, Luana admitted to herself. It was Greg. Well, if she was being perfectly honest, it was the combination of Greg *and* Phoebe. The two were like oil and water. *I hope we don't end up with Greg as our client. Working with him and Phoebe together would be unbearable.*

Phoebe's jaw dropped. "Who does Heather think she is, Princess Kate?"

"Actually, Kate's proper title is Duchess of Cambridge," said Mary Beth.

Phoebe looked at the ceiling and gave an exaggerated sigh. Mary Beth was forever spouting useless information. "Who cares?"

"Heather has a valid point," said Luana. "We don't need the judge until we're ready to begin the trial. We need to decide who is going to represent whom."

"Why can't we do it like we did in the last case?" Lindsey spoke for the first time since the older boys' arrival. "It worked well enough for the Corbett trial." She forced herself to keep her head up when the children turned their attention to her, even though her heart fluttered in her chest like a caged bird.

"We could do that. But I thought it would be fairer to give Declan and Greg the choice of who they want to represent them," said Luana.

"I'd be happy to represent Greg. I'm already an

experienced plaintiff's attorney," said Mary Beth airily, referring to the Kids' Court's previous case, in which she had represented her best friend, Jenny.

Phoebe stifled her laughter. "You've tried *one* case, Mary Beth. I'd hardly call that experienced."

"I'm not claiming to be Ally McBeal or anything like that," said Mary Beth.

"Who?" Phoebe scrunched up her nose.

"You've never heard of Ally McBeal?" Mary Beth blinked.

Phoebe stared back at her, a blank expression on her face.

"She's an amazing lawyer on television," said Mary Beth.

Phoebe rolled her eyes. She should have known Ally Mc-whoever was a TV character. Obsessed with courtroom dramas, Mary Beth watched them nonstop and constantly compared real life to her beloved shows.

"I'm good with Mary Beth being Greg's lawyer. I want Luana to represent me." Declan thought since Luana had done such a good job representing Jimmy, he wanted her on his side.

"Is that OK with you, Greg?" asked Luana.

Greg gave Mary Beth a once-over. "Are you sure

you know what you're doing?"

"Yes, of course I do." Mary Beth stuck her nose in the air and sniffed. "I've already tried an actual case; I've watched hundreds of episodes of TV court shows, and I'm quite familiar with courtroom procedure."

Phoebe snickered. She remembered Mary Beth's first attempt at being a lawyer. Her "hundreds of episodes of TV court shows" hadn't helped her then. Her first try at direct examination had been disastrous. Phoebe had laughed so hard she'd almost peed herself.

"Well, if you're sure you know what you're doing, I'm OK with you being my lawyer," said Greg.

Mary Beth beamed approvingly at him as though he'd just paid her the highest compliment. "Of course you are. It always amazes people how much I know about courts and stuff."

"I'm sure." Sarcasm laced Greg's voice, but Mary Beth continued beaming at him.

Ashley facepalmed. Her sister was so oblivious sometimes.

Luana sighed. She hoped this case wouldn't be too much trouble. Greg wasn't a bad kid, but he could rub people the wrong way when he wanted.

THE GO-KARTASTROPHE

Who was she kidding? He rubbed people the wrong way even when he wasn't trying!

"OK, everyone, why don't I tell the boys our roles in the court?" said Luana. "Ashley is the private investigator on Greg's legal team, Phoebe on Declan's team. Jake is our bailiff, Lindsey is our court reporter, and you already know Mary Beth and I are lawyers. Finally, Heather Crandall is our judge."

"*Ahem*. I'd like to say something, Luana." Jake planted his feet in a wide stance and folded his arms across his chest.

"Sure, Jake, go ahead."

"As Luana just told you, I'm the bailiff. I hope you both plan on behaving yourselves because I wouldn't want to have to throw you out of court." He uncrossed his arms and flexed his right bicep while giving the two older boys a meaningful look.

"No problem, Jake. I promise to behave," Greg choked out, trying hard not to laugh.

"Me, too." Declan grinned.

"Thanks, Jake," said Luana. "If there's nothing else we need to talk about, I think we're ready to begin just as soon as we can get Heather on board. I'll text her and let her know we're a go." She pulled out her cell phone and tapped out a message.

Within seconds, she received a response. "Heather says she can start in the morning. Does that work for everyone?"

All the children agreed they were available.

"OK, perfect. I'll see you all then," said Luana.

CHAPTER 3

Court is in Session

HEATHER CRANDALL'S TALL, gangly frame sailed into the courtroom. Thick, red curls flowed around her shoulders, and a sprinkle of freckles stood out on her pale cheeks. "Good morning, everyone." The thirteen-year-old looked down her upturned nose with a slight smile on her lips as she addressed the mostly eleven-year-old group.

"Oh hey, Heather," said Phoebe. "I like your new braces. Cool color!"

"Thanks." Heather grinned, revealing the neon-pink braces on her teeth. "So, what's the case about?"

"Didn't Jake tell you?" Phoebe asked.

Heather snorted. "No. He wouldn't tell me anything! He said if I'd wanted to know, I should have come to the meeting." She pressed her lips together.

Phoebe chuckled. *Good for Jake.*

Luana bit back a smile. Although she'd told Heather the court had a case, she had not given her any details. "It's Declan and Greg. You know, the wrecked go-kart issue."

"No surprise there." Like most of the neighborhood, Heather was aware of the boys' ongoing argument over what—or who—had caused the go-kart crash. "Are we ready to begin?"

Luana's eyes scanned the courtroom. "I think so. It looks like we're all here."

"Good." Heather's eyes found where the boys were in the courtroom. Declan sat at the defense table, chatting with Phoebe, while Greg stood by the plaintiff's table, listening to whatever Mary Beth was saying. Heather smiled when she noticed the dazed expression on Greg's face. She could relate. Listening to Mary Beth often left Heather feeling dazed and confused. "OK, everyone, let's take our seats and get started. Declan, Greg, welcome to the Kids' Court."

Shuffling sounds emitted throughout the courtroom as the children scrambled to their seats. They had arranged the room to resemble a real court as much as possible. Heather's battered desk, which served as her judge's bench, sat at the front,

THE GO-KARTASTROPHE

facing the rest of the court. Lindsey's toddler-sized table and chair stood on Heather's right, facing Heather and the others at an angle. Witnesses sat on Heather's left in an old kitchen chair while testifying.

The plaintiff and defense desks—two folding tables—stood side by side, with an old audio-visual cart between them that the children used as a lectern.

"Before we get started, Luana, would you tell the boys the court rules so they understand how we do things?" said Heather.

"Sure." Luana twisted in her seat to see Greg sitting at the plaintiff's table with Mary Beth and Ashley on the other side of the lectern. Declan sat at the defense table with her and Phoebe. "OK, here's a quick rundown of the basics. First, always address Heather, the judge, as Your Honor. The rest of us address each other as miss or mister with our first names. So you two will be Mr. Greg and Mr. Declan. Second, never speak while the judge is speaking and *never* argue with her. And third, stand when speaking to the court." She gestured to the AV cart. "Mary Beth and I stand there at the lectern when questioning witnesses. That's pretty much it. Questions?"

"Yeah," said Greg. "What's a lectern?"

Phoebe shook her head. "Duh. It's a podium, dumbo. You know. That thing people stand behind and put their notes on when making speeches."

Greg shot her a dirty look. "That"—he pointed to the AV cart—"doesn't look like any podium I've ever seen." He returned his attention to Luana. "And another question: how do you speak to the court? The court isn't a person."

"It kinda is," said Luana. "The judge is the court. It makes sense if you think about it. We say things like 'the court ruled,' 'the court decided,' and 'the court's decision.' If the court wasn't a person, it couldn't do any of those things."

"I never thought about it that way before," said Greg.

"Any other questions?" Luana's eyes moved from Greg to Declan, but both boys shook their heads.

"OK, great. So we can get started." Heather rapped the gavel once on her desk. It was a wooden toy replica of gavels used by judges, which Mr. Porcello had given to Luana years earlier. "The Kids' Court is now in session! We're here to decide the case of Greg Foster versus Declan Mathias. Mr. Greg claims Mr. Declan crashed and wrecked his

THE GO-KARTASTROPHE

go-cart. Mr. Declan admits he crashed the go-cart but says the accident was not his fault. Are you ready to begin, Miss Mary Beth?"

"I am, Your Honor." Mary Beth stood up and pranced to the lectern. "I call Greg Foster to the witness chair."

"Mr. Greg, please come forward and stand here." Heather gestured to a spot in front of the witness chair. "Bailiff, you may give the witness the oath."

Jake swaggered forward, puffing his chest out to draw attention to the shiny, metallic sheriff's badge he wore. "Please raise your right hand."

Greg raised his hand.

"Do you promise to tell the truth, the whole truth, and nothing but the truth?"

"I do."

"Thank you, Deputy Jake," said Heather. "Mr. Greg, please sit. Miss Mary Beth, you may begin your direct examination."

"Hold up. Timeout." Greg tapped the palm of his right hand against the tops of his left fingers in the timeout signal. "What's a direct examination?"

"Well, it's nothing to do with going to the doctor if that's what you're thinking," said Jake.

Greg stared at Jake with a bemused expression on his face. "I didn't think that at all."

"Oh. That's what I thought the first time I heard it." Red color stained Jake's cheeks.

Heather rolled her eyes. "That's because you're a dufus, Jake."

"I am not!" He glared at his sister.

"Guys, let's not fight," said Luana. "Greg, a direct examination is when a lawyer questions a witness he brought to court. When the other lawyer questions the witness, it's a cross-examination."

"Is that the only difference between the two?" asked Greg. "I don't get why they have different names."

"Well, lawyers can only ask open-ended questions like who, what, where, when, and how during a direct examination," said Luana. "Open-ended questions allow the witness to tell a story to the court. Cross-examination involves very pointed, specific questions that suggest a yes or no answer. We call those leading questions. Lawyers

THE GO-KARTASTROPHE

can ask leading and open-ended questions during cross-examination, but most stick to leading questions. It's a strategy thing."

"Like running different plays in sports." Greg nodded. "Thanks for clearing that up."

"You're welcome."

"OK, Mr. Greg," said Heather. "If you're all set, your lawyer can get started."

"I am."

"Very good. Go ahead, Miss Mary Beth."

"Thanks, Heather, er, I mean, Your Honor. Good morning, Greg—Mr. Greg."

"Good morning."

"You're the owner of a—er—a . . . um . . . a go-thingy?" Mary Beth wrinkled her forehead.

"It's a go-kart," said Greg. "And yes, I own one."

Mary Beth flushed. "Er—thanks. I couldn't remember what you called it."

Phoebe shook her head in disbelief. "How could she forget go-kart?" She leaned across Declan, sitting between them, to whisper to Luana. "The entire case is about a go-kart accident."

A smile tugged at Luana's lips, and she gave a half-shrug. She was used to Mary Beth's absent-mindedness.

"Tell us about your go-kart, Mr. Greg," said Mary

Beth.

"It's a motorized vehicle my dad and I built together. I planned to enter it in the annual Tri-County Go-Kart Race-A-Thon, but now I probably won't be able to, thanks to Declan."

"Why not?" asked Mary Beth.

"Because, for one, it's damaged, and I don't have the money to fix it," said Greg. "And then there's the fact that my mom is against me entering the race since the accident."

"Was she OK with you entering the race before the accident?"

"Yes. Sort of. My mom doesn't like go-karts. She never has. My dad raced as a kid, and I've always wanted to race too, but Mom refused to let me. She didn't even want me to have a go-kart. It wasn't until last summer that she let me have one. Mom's an emergency room nurse and sees a lot of nasty stuff. It makes her worry. She says the ER gets tons of patients with race-related injuries during the Race-A-Thon every year."

"Why did she agree to let you race this year?" asked Mary Beth.

"Dad and I have been working on her forever, and we finally got her to allow me to enter. I had to remind her I'm thirteen now, hardly a baby!" Greg

THE GO-KARTASTROPHE

snorted. "Dad entered his first go-kart race when he was nine and was only ten when he won his first Race-A-Thon title. He won the best overall go-kart driver award for the ten to twelve-year-old division. Nowadays, they won't let you enter until you're ten, but I've already missed three years of racing time." He made another sound of disgust.

"Anyhow, Mom agreed to let me race. She was still worried about it, but she knows I've been practicing hard this past year, and not to brag, but I am an excellent driver."

Phoebe turned her head toward Declan and Luana and stuck her finger in her mouth, pretending to gag herself.

Declan chuckled, and Luana shook her head. "Behave, Pheebs," she murmured, biting her lip to prevent a smile.

Phoebe crossed her eyes and stuck out her tongue at Luana before returning her attention to the trial. Luana rolled her eyes at her friend's silliness.

"After Declan crashed the kart, Mom changed her mind," said Greg. "She's decided it's a sign from God I shouldn't enter the race and says she's just thankful Declan didn't get hurt. She won't listen to a word I have to say. Even if I get the kart fixed in time, I doubt she'll let me race now." He glowered at Declan. "You've ruined everything!"

"That's too bad about your mom, Greg," said Mary Beth. "From everything you've said, I take it you know the defendant, Declan Mathias?"

Greg stared slack-jawed at Mary Beth. "Yeah, you could say we're acquainted."

Phoebe snickered. So much for Mary Beth's claim that she was "experienced."

"How long have you known him?"

"Six years."

"How well do you know Declan?"

"He's my best friend. At least, he used to be. That was before he crashed my go-kart and refused to pay for the repairs."

Declan gritted his teeth.

Sensing his frustration, Phoebe threw Declan a warning glance. "Relax."

His jaw hardened, but he nodded and sat back in the chair, folding his arms across his chest as he listened to Greg's testimony.

"When did Declan crash your go-kart?" said Mary Beth.

"Last Thursday."

"Where was the accident?"

"Over at the trails."

THE GO-KARTASTROPHE

"The trails?" Mary Beth cocked her head. "Where's that?"

"You've never been to the trails?" Greg's eyebrows rose. "They're on the other side of the conservation land, past the woods. It's mostly dirt tracks, but kids ride their bikes and stuff back there. Some adults use it too. Anyhow, that's where I take my go-kart when I want to give it a good run."

"Was Declan driving your go-kart when he crashed it?"

"Huh?" Greg facepalmed. "What kind of question is that? Of course he was driving. How else could he have crashed it?"

Mary Beth's ears turned red. "Er—yes. Go—good point." She cleared her throat. "Um, you—you were telling us how Declan crashed the cart."

Greg let out a heavy sigh. "We took the kart out for a practice run. I've been doing that since I built it a couple of months ago. After I drove a few laps around the course, Declan asked for a go. I'd let him drive it before, so I thought nothing of it. Obviously, I made a mistake. He didn't know what he was doing and wrecked my kart."

"I told you the accident wasn't my fault!" Declan sprang to his feet, moving with such force his chair clattered to the floor behind him. "There was something wrong with the go-kart. It didn't respond to the steering."

"Order in the court!" Heather repeatedly thumped the gavel on her desk. "Mr. Declan, sit down and be quiet, or I'll have the bailiff remove you from my courtroom."

Luana placed a hand on his arm. "Please try to control yourself, Declan. I know it's frustrating, but you'll get to tell your side later."

"Sorry." He reached down and righted his chair, then slumped into it. Stretching his legs out before him, he crossed his ankles. A muscle in his jaw twitched.

"It's OK." Luana patted his arm and switched her focus to the court. "I'm sorry for my client's outburst, Your Honor. This situation is—er, difficult for him. It won't happen again."

"See that it doesn't, Miss Luana," said Heather. "You may continue, Miss Mary Beth."

"Thanks," said Mary Beth. "Where were you when Declan was driving the go-kart?"

"I was standing beside the track."

"Could you see Declan from where you were standing?"

"Most of the time."

THE GO-KARTASTROPHE

"Could you see him when the accident happened?"

"Yes. Declan was coming around a curve in the track. He was driving fast. He wrenched the steering wheel, and the kart spun out of control. It ran off the trail and hit a tree."

"Your Honor, I need to introduce a piece of evidence." Mary Beth pursed her lips. "Um, we have to label it, right? For identification, I mean."

"Yes," said Heather. "And since it's your first item of evidence, it will be plaintiff's A."

In trials, courts assign an identifying number or letter to each piece of evidence. The Kids' Court labeled the plaintiff's evidence with letters and the defense's with numbers.

"What's the evidence?" asked Heather.

"Just a moment, Heath—I mean, Your Honor." Mary Beth moved toward the door that led out to the yard. "I'll need Greg to help me."

Greg got to his feet and followed as Mary Beth exited the courtroom. Several minutes passed, but neither Mary Beth nor Greg returned.

After a while, the children grew impatient when the two had still not reappeared. *Where was Mary Beth, and what was she up to now?*

CHAPTER 4

Tireless Testimony

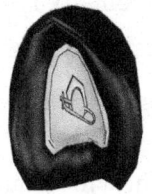

SEVERAL MORE MINUTES passed before Mary Beth finally returned, red-faced and panting. "Jake, we need your help."

Jake followed her out of the courtroom. A few minutes later, when they reappeared, Jake and Greg were half-dragging, half-carrying a smashed-up go-kart between them, while Mary Beth called out instructions.

"Careful, Jake. You almost hit the wall!"

"Stop being so bossy," Jake snarled. "*You* were too weak to move it, remember?"

"I wasn't too weak. I'm just not as, you know, hefty as you are."

Jake's eyes shot daggers at her.

"Where'd you have that hidden?" asked Phoebe. "I didn't see it when I arrived, and I got here after you did."

Mary Beth gave her a satisfied smile. "It was right outside the door. I covered it with a tarp. That's why you didn't notice it."

Once the boys had placed the go-kart in the court's well—the open area between the judge's bench and counsel tables—Greg returned to his seat, and Mary Beth continued with her direct examination.

"Mr. Greg, I'm showing you what the court has identified as plaintiff's A." She gestured to the go-kart. "Do you recognize it?"

"Yes, I do."

"What is it?"

"It's my go-kart. Or what's left of it."

"Was this how your go-kart looked before you loaned it to Declan?"

Greg snorted. "Of course not. It was in pristine condition when I let him drive it. That"—he pointed at the go-kart—"is how it looked *after* Declan wrecked it."

"Can you please describe how the go-cart looks now?"

"Why?" He raised his eyebrows. "Everyone can see it."

"Because we have to add details about every piece of evidence to the court record," said

THE GO-KARTASTROPHE

Heather. "Including what it is and how it looks. But Lindsey can only type what she hears, not what she sees. So, you describe the go-kart, and she types what you say."

"Oh. OK, let's see." Greg tilted his head to one side and studied the go-kart as he spoke. "The cart hit the tree head-on at a good speed, so the front end smashed in. The chassis and front axle are bent, the steering column broke off, and the right tire is totaled." He sighed and ran a hand over his face.

"Have you priced how much it would cost to fix the go-kart?" Mary Beth leaned against the lectern, resting her forearms on its surface, and fluttered her flip-flop against her right heel. It made a loud flapping sound in the quiet courtroom. When Mary Beth noticed the annoyed glance Heather sent her way, she quickly straightened, planting both feet firmly on the floor.

"Not exactly, but I have a pretty good idea. It cost close to a thousand dollars to build. It could have cost a lot less, but we only used the best materials. I'd estimate around two hundred dollars for the repairs." Greg ran his fingers through his hair, pushing it back from his forehead. "I need a new tire and new steel to replace the steering column and front axle. I'm hoping I'll be able to straighten out the chassis, but I think that might be a pipe dream. It's in terrible shape. I'll probably have to replace parts of the frame. I won't know for sure until I start the work."

"So, two hundred dollars, you think?"

"More or less."

"Thank you, Mr. Greg." Mary Beth beamed. "I'm done with this witness, Your Honor."

"Excuse me, Your Honor," said Luana.

"Yes, Miss Luana, I know it's your turn to question Mr. Greg," said Heather.

"It's not that. Could you ask the witness to explain the unfamiliar words he just used to describe the go-kart? I have no clue what a—er—chassis is."

"Good point. I admit I was a little lost myself. Mr. Greg, those parts you mentioned?" Heather swiveled in her chair to face Lindsey. "Miss Lindsey, can you read back the go-kart parts Mr. Greg just mentioned?"

"No problem, Your Honor." Focusing on her computer screen, Lindsey read, "'The cart hit the tree head-on at a good speed, so the front end smashed in. The chassis and front axle are bent, the steering column broke off, and the right tire is totaled.'"

THE GO-KARTASTROPHE

"Thank you, Miss Lindsey," said Heather. "Mr. Greg, please show us where the various parts you mentioned are on the go-kart and explain—explain . . ." She threw her hands up in the air. "Oh, just tell us what you mean by each word or whatever."

"No problem." Greg smirked. "But now you all get how I feel when you throw your big legal words around. It's no fun when you don't understand what people are talking about, is it?"

"Just get on with the explanation already!" Phoebe growled.

Greg winked at her, then standing up, he sauntered over to the vehicle and pointed to its front section. "This is the front end that hit the tree. As you can see, it's smashed in. The chassis is the go-kart's frame. You build that first, then add the other parts, tires, steering wheel, etc." He flipped the kart to lay it on its side. "This is the front axle." He pointed to a metal rod that ran from left to right across the front end of the go-kart. "The front tires attach to the front axle."

"Where's the right tire?" Jake had been paying rapt attention to Greg's description of the go-kart.

"I left it at home." Greg looked at Mary Beth. "I guess we should have brought the tire to court, too, huh?"

Mary Beth nodded, her cheeks heating to a deep shade of pink. She hadn't thought to bring the tire to court.

"Anyway, this is the steering column." Greg pointed to a steel rod that ran from the front axle up through a hole in the go-kart floor. "The steering wheel attaches to it at the top. The steering column should attach to the front axle, but as you can see, it's broken." He looked around at the others. "That's it in a nutshell."

"Thank you, Mr. Greg," said Heather. "Miss Luana, I assume you intend to cross-examine Mr. Greg?"

"Yes, Your Honor. But before I begin, I was wondering if—"

"Let me guess. You'd like a short recess to examine the go-kart?" A smile tugged at Heather's lips.

Luana chuckled. "Yes, I would, Your Honor. Thank you."

"Very well." Heather glanced at her watch. "It's almost one. I say we break now and resume after lunch." She banged the gavel. "Court is in recess."

❖ ❖ ❖

Declan stooped next to Phoebe and watched as

she examined the go-kart. "What are you looking for?"

"Clues."

He glanced at Luana, eyebrows raised, as if to say, *what clues?* Luana shrugged and shook her head.

Phoebe was in her element when trying to decipher a problem or solve a puzzle. There was nothing she liked better. Her dream was to be a detective like her father, Robert Chen. Mr. Chen was the chief of detectives at the Oakdale Police Department.

Phoebe continued examining the go-kart in silence for a while. "Hmm." She ran her hand over the kart's bent frame. "Greg's right. This thing is in terrible shape. He's sure he can fix it?"

"Yeah," said Declan. "Greg's great with his hands, and so is Matt. Their dad taught them. Mr. Foster says if he hadn't gone to engineering school, he would have been a mechanic or a carpenter. There's nothing he can't build!"

"Yeah, Mr. Foster sure is handy," Luana agreed. "He helped my dad build our storage shed when we moved in a few years ago. Daddy decided to build it himself, even though Mom wanted him to hire someone." She shook her head. "It turned out not to be as easy as Daddy thought it would be, but thankfully, Mr. Foster came to his rescue." She giggled at the memory. "Mom said it did not surprise her Daddy needed help. She says Daddy's brilliant and good at a lot of stuff, but he is *not* handy!"

As the two talked, Phoebe continued examining the go-kart. After a few moments, she reached into her mini-backpack and pulled out a magnifying glass. She leaned closer to the kart and ran her hand over the metal frame. "Hey, guys, check this out."

Luana and Declan moved closer to the kart to see better.

"What is it?" asked Luana.

THE GO-KARTASTROPHE

"See this pink mark on the steering column and front axle?"

Luana leaned in and peered at the mark to which Phoebe pointed. "Yes, I see it."

Declan squinted. "What is that?"

"I was hoping you'd be able to tell us," said Phoebe.

Declan shook his head. "I dunno. Greg used nothing pink when he built the go-kart."

"Well, whatever it is, it looks out of place," said Luana.

"Feel this." Phoebe ran her hand over the bottom edge of the steering column, where it had broken off from the front axle. "It's weird. Part of the edge is smooth, but the rest is pretty rough."

Luana kneeled and ran her fingers around the edge of the broken steering column. "You're right, Pheebs. One part feels smooth, almost silky, while the rest is jagged. What do you think it means?"

Phoebe shrugged. "I dunno. It could be nothing."

Luana got to her feet, releasing a breath. "Hopefully, we'll figure it out as the case continues. Now, how about we get something to eat? I'm starving!" She brushed her hands on her denim capris, removing the debris they had picked up from the go-cart. "Would you like to stay for lunch,

Declan? It's Rosie's specialty, jerk chicken. It's delicious!" Rosie was the Porcellos' longtime housekeeper and, like Luana's mother, was from Jamaica. Her cooking was legendary in the neighborhood.

"Rosie made jerk chicken?" Phoebe's eyes bugged. "Why didn't you say that earlier?" She jumped to her feet and sprinted toward the door, intent on getting upstairs as quickly as possible. "First one upstairs gets dibs on the chicken!"

Declan grinned. "I'm guessing Phoebe likes Rosie's jerk chicken, huh?"

Luana held her thumb and index finger a smidge apart. "Just a teeny bit."

They laughed as they hurried after Phoebe, eager to get their share of jerk chicken before the pint-sized firebrand devoured it all.

CHAPTER 5

Hard as Nails

"OK, EVERYONE, COURT is in session." Heather sat down at the judge's bench. "Miss Luana, are you ready to begin your cross-examination?"

"I am, Your Honor."

"Mr. Greg, please return to the witness chair so we can get started." Heather fixed Greg with emerald-green eyes as he sat down. "Remember, you're still under oath."

"OK."

"Mr. Greg," said Luana, "you testified you and your dad built the go-kart. Is that correct?"

"Yes." Greg nodded.

"He helped you with the entire project, from start to finish?"

"No, not really. Dad drew up the plans for the go-kart. He and I bought all the materials together, and he helped me build the frame. But then he got busy at work, so I continued without him. He checked my progress from time to time and offered advice when I needed it, which wasn't often."

"Did anyone else help you?"

"Yeah, Matt helped some," said Greg, referring to his ten-year-old brother. "And Declan did, too."

"Would you say you were the one who was in charge of the project?" asked Luana.

"Yeah, I guess."

"When you finished the go-kart, did your dad inspect it?"

"Yes."

"Did he find anything wrong with it?"

Greg gave her a superior smile. "There was nothing wrong for him to find."

"When did you finish the go-kart?"

"A few weeks ago."

"And that's when your dad inspected it, right?" said Luana.

"Yeah."

"Has he inspected it since?"

"Why would he?" Greg arched an eyebrow.

Luana sighed. *I hope Greg won't be difficult.* "Please answer my question. Has your dad inspected the go-kart since that first time?"

"No. There was no reason for him to inspect it

again."

"Has he driven it?"

"Once or twice after I first built it."

"But not since?"

"No."

"What about you?"

"What about me?" Greg reclined in his chair and propped his right foot on the opposite knee.

Luana gritted her teeth. "Have you inspected the go-kart since you first built it?"

"Depends on what you mean by 'inspect.' I've looked it over from time to time, checked the brakes, the tires, that sort of thing."

"What about the day of the crash? Did you look it over that day?"

"As a matter of fact, I did, and there was nothing wrong with it."

Luana froze. "You did?"

"I did." Greg gave her a smug smile. "You can ask Matt. He was there."

"Why didn't you mention this before?"

"Nobody asked me. Besides, I didn't think it was important. The fact is, I drove the kart myself right before I let Declan have a go. It performed perfectly. I could tell there was nothing wrong with it."

"I see." Luana twirled a dark braid around her finger, chewing on her lower lip as she tried to gather her thoughts. *Think, Luana! Think!* "What exactly did you check the day of the accident?" she asked finally.

"What I always check," said Greg. "The tires, the brakes, and the steering."

"You checked the steering?" Luana's voice was little more than a squeak.

"Yes, I did. Like I said, you can ask Matt. He was there."

"Was that the first time you took the go-kart out?" asked Luana.

"Hardly. I've been practicing for the upcoming race since I finished the kart a couple of months ago. I took it out several times a week. And before you ask, it performed perfectly each time I drove it.

THE GO-KARTASTROPHE

You can ask Matt about that, too. He usually went with me whenever I practiced."

"What about my client?"

"What about him?" Greg smirked and folded his arms across his chest.

Luana propped one elbow on the lectern and massaged her forehead with the heel of her hand. She drew in a deep breath, then slowly exhaled. Greg seemed to be doing his best to make things difficult for her. "Had Declan been out with you before the day of the crash?"

"Yes, a few times."

"Did he drive the go-kart any of those times?"

"Yes." Greg's smirk vanished.

"How many times before the accident had Declan driven your go-kart?"

"I'm not sure."

"More than once?" asked Luana.

"Yes."

"More than twice?"

"Yes." By this time, Greg had lowered his foot to the floor, uncrossed his arms, and sat upright, his eyes wide and alert.

Luana leaned forward, gripping the edge of the lectern, and pinned Greg with her eyes. "Would you say it was over five times?"

"Yes."

"Over ten?"

"OK . . . yes. Yes! All right?" Greg raked his fingers through his blond hair. "He drove it several times. Maybe a dozen or more. I can't remember exactly. Satisfied?"

A smile played around Luana's lips. "So, before the day of the crash, my client drove your go-kart at least a dozen times, correct?"

"Yes." Greg pressed his lips together so hard they almost disappeared.

"And before the day of the crash, my client had never damaged your go-kart, correct?"

"No, he hadn't."

"He never had an accident during any of those many times he drove the go-kart?" she persisted.

"No." Greg spoke through clenched teeth.

"You testified you were waiting beside the track while Declan was driving the go-kart. Is that right?"

"Yes." Greg gave a jerky nod of his head.

"You also testified that from where you were standing, you could see Declan on the track 'most of the time,' correct?"

"Yes."

"When you say you could see him 'most of the time,' that means sometimes you could not see him.

Isn't that right?" Luana arched an eyebrow.

"Yes, but there were only a few brief moments when I couldn't see him."

"Isn't it true the trails have a lot of twists and turns?"

"Yes, it's a winding trail."

"Then how could you see Declan most of the time?"

"If you were familiar with the area," Greg retorted, "you would know it's hilly. I was standing in a raised area. That's where I was as I watched Dec drive."

"I see. So, you weren't beside the track as you led us to believe, right?"

"Er—no. Not exactly." Greg crossed his legs, then immediately uncrossed them.

"You were looking down at Declan, correct?"

"Pretty much. Declan crashed into a tree almost directly below me, so I was looking down at him when the accident happened."

"Earlier, you said Declan was going fast as he came around that last curve before the crash. Do you know how fast he was going?"

"Don't you mean 'Mr. Declan'?" Greg taunted.

"Excuse me?" Luana knitted her brows.

"You've been calling him Declan. Aren't you

supposed to call him Mr. Declan?"

Luana ground her jaw. *I'm beginning to understand why Phoebe dislikes this boy so much.* "Fine. *Mr.* Declan. Now, can you please answer my question?"

"Could you repeat it? I don't remember what you asked." A corner of Greg's mouth quirked up.

Luana gave a heavy sigh. "How fast was *Mr.* Declan driving when he drove around that last curve?"

"I dunno." He shrugged.

"Could you perhaps estimate how fast he was driving? Unless, of course, you're unable to estimate speed."

Greg narrowed his eyes. "Of course I can estimate speed. He was traveling somewhere between twenty and twenty-five miles per hour. For sure, no faster than twenty-five miles per hour."

"As a prudent driver, I assume you drive around that curve much slower, don't you?"

"Hardly," said Greg. "I drive around those curves at speeds of at least thirty-five or forty miles per hour."

"In that case, Declan's—I'm sorry, *Mr.* Declan's— speed of about twenty-five miles per hour was not too fast, was it?"

Greg's eyes bulged. He opened his mouth, then closed it. Opened, closed, opened, then closed, looking like a fish in an aquarium.

Greg realized he'd walked into Luana's neatly set trap. He had no choice but to answer her question with a no; otherwise, he'd look like a complete idiot. "No, Declan's speed wasn't too fast," he grudgingly admitted.

"So, it would be safe to say the speed he was driving was not a cause of the accident, correct?"

Greg wet his lips and threaded his right fingers into his hair. "Um . . . yes." Rallying, he added, "The speed might not have been a cause of the accident, but his driving was. He wrenched the steering wheel so hard I'm surprised it didn't pop right off. That's what caused him to lose control of the kart." He sat back and gave her a self-satisfied smile.

"I didn't lose control!" Declan bolted from his chair and rushed forward, stopping a few feet away from Greg, hands fisted, his lips drawn back in a snarl. "You know what, Greg? I'm sick and tired of you saying I caused the crash. It was your wretched go-kart. It's a piece of cra–"

"That's enough, Declan!" Heather banged the gavel repeatedly. "Get control of yourself and sit back down." The look she gave him was so ferocious he took a step backward.

Jake, who had jumped up when Declan dashed forward and now stood hovering between the two boys, looked as though he wanted to be anywhere else but was ready to step in if necessary.

"Sorry." Declan let out a harsh breath and rolled his shoulders. "He just makes me so mad!"

"I understand. But we're here to find the truth about what caused the accident," said Heather. "We can't do that if you keep losing it."

Greg hadn't moved a muscle when Declan came running toward him. He lounged in his chair with one arm slung over its back, regarding Declan with a smug expression.

Declan scowled at him before returning to his seat.

"Finish up, Luana," said Heather, "before they come to blows."

"Good idea." Luana quickly resumed her cross-examination. "Mr. Greg, you said you saw when Declan wrenched the steering wheel. In which direction did he turn it?"

"Hmm." Greg closed his eyes and considered her question, then reopened them. "He pulled it to the right."

THE GO-KARTASTROPHE

"Are you sure?"

"Yes, I'm positive." Greg gave a firm nod of his head. "He pulled it to the right."

"During our examination of the go-kart, we noticed a pink mark on the front axle. Do you know what it is?"

Greg shrugged. "I don't know. I noticed it right after the crash when I checked out the kart and assumed something at the trails got on it."

"The go-kart's frame is twisted, not broken. Isn't that right?"

"That's right."

"Did you use the same type of steel to make the frame and the steering column?"

"Yes. I bought several lengths of steel and cut them down into the sizes I needed to make the frame, steering column, front axle, etc. It's pretty easy."

"Thank you, Mr. Greg." Luana gave him a tight smile. He had been such a tiresome witness. "I have no more questions, Your Honor." *Thank goodness.*

"Excellent!" Heather glanced at her watch. "This is a perfect time to adjourn for the day." At Greg's puzzled expression, she explained, "Adjourn means to take a break." She banged the gavel. "Court is adjourned. We'll resume in the morning."

CHAPTER 6

A Colorful Witness

"HOW'S YOUR CASE going?" Luana's mom asked. Renee Porcello was an attractive, brown-skinned woman with dark, kinky curls and pretty brown eyes. Bright sunlight pouring in through a large window overlooking the backyard enhanced the natural reddish highlights in her hair. Mrs. Porcello was a Jamaican native who had lived in the United States for many years and spoke with a slight, lilting accent.

"I'm not sure," said Luana. She and her mother were having breakfast in the informal dining room—a cozy area separated from the kitchen by a half-wall. "At first, I thought it was going great, but I got a nasty surprise yesterday when I cross-examined Greg."

"Greg is the plaintiff, isn't he?" Like Luana's father, Mrs. Porcello was an attorney. However, she did not work for a government agency as her husband did. Instead, Mrs. Porcello was in private practice and partnered with another lawyer.

"Yeah, he is. He says Declan caused the crash that wrecked his go-kart and wants him to pay for the repairs."

"What was the nasty surprise?"

"Greg says Declan caused the crash when he yanked the steering wheel and lost control of the go-kart. Declan says it wasn't his fault. He insists there was something wrong with the steering. The problem is Greg says he checked the steering himself before taking the go-kart out that day. He also drove the vehicle around the trails a few times before Declan drove it. According to Greg, it worked perfectly." Luana grimaced, remembering Greg's cocky attitude during his cross-examination.

Just then, David Porcello came strolling in. "Good morning, lovely ladies!" He was a tall man with hazel eyes that invariably twinkled with mischief. When he smiled—which was more often than not—dimples, reminiscent of his daughter's, appeared on both cheeks.

"Hey, Dad. You're bright and chipper this morning." Luana glanced at the clock hanging above the doorway. "And you're late."

THE GO-KARTASTROPHE

He kissed her on the cheek. "Which is why I'm bright and chipper. But I'm not late, not really. Judge Marshal had an appointment and couldn't resume court until ten. I didn't need to be in the office this morning, so I got to sleep in for a change." He sat down on the bench next to Luana and helped himself to bacon and eggs from platters on the picnic-style dining table. "How's your case going?"

Luana smiled. "You and Mom think alike. She just asked me the same thing."

"And?" he prompted.

She sighed. "Not too good."

"She cross-examined the plaintiff yesterday and discovered some information that's bad for her client," Mrs. Porcello explained. "She needs to weaken his testimony, or she may lose the trial."

Quickly, Luana gave him the details.

"Hmm." Her father pursed his lips. "Did you ask Greg to describe how he checked the steering? There are different ways of doing it, you know. From simply spinning the steering wheel to ensure the tires turn appropriately to a complete undercarriage inspection."

"Really?" said Luana. "I—I didn't ask Greg to describe what he did. I was so surprised when he said he'd inspected the go-kart I couldn't think straight. I'm not much of a lawyer, am I?" Her shoulders sagged.

"Don't be so hard on yourself, honey." Mrs. Porcello patted her hand. "I'm sure you're doing a great job. Even experienced lawyers make mistakes sometimes. And believe me, we've all had our share of nasty surprises in court!"

"Tell me about it," said David Porcello. "Just last week, I had a witness testify to something completely different from what he'd told me in an earlier interview." He winced at the memory. "Talk about surprised. Anyway, I'm sure you'll annihilate Greg's testimony." He waved a butter knife in one hand, pretending to be involved in a sword fight.

Luana laughed at her father's theatrics and shook her head. *Annihilate, meaning to destroy,* she thought. *I'll have to use that one to annoy Phoebe.* She grinned to herself, imagining her friend's reaction. Phoebe often scolded Luana for using "non-kid friendly" vocabulary. "That's asking a lot, Daddy," she said. "Especially as I know absolutely nothing about go-karts! You should have heard Greg yesterday talking about axles, steering columns, and chas–chas–"

"Chassis?" Mr. Porcello grinned.

THE GO-KARTASTROPHE

"Yes, that's it. Why a person can't just say frame, I'll never know. Why is everything so complicated?"

Mrs. Porcello chuckled. "Now you know how other people feel when we use terms like preponderance, proffer, and other legal words."

"That's what Greg said!"

"Never fear, my dear," said Mr. Porcello. "You may know nothing about go-karts, but you'll figure it out. After all, you're like your father—resourceful and smart."

Renee Porcello rolled her eyes. "Yes, just like her father. *I* certainly had nothing to do with it."

"Of course you did, dear." His hazel eyes twinkled. "She got her beauty from you."

Luana giggled. Sometimes her parents were so silly. But they were right; she would figure it out. She had to—Declan was counting on her. "I'd love to stick around and listen to you two banter all day, but court will be in session soon, and I'm supposed to meet Phoebe and Declan early. They'll be here any minute. Gotta go." She gave both her parents a quick kiss and dashed out of the room.

❖ ❖ ❖

"What's the plan for today?" Declan sat at the defense table with Luana and Phoebe.

"I'm not sure yet," said Luana. "It depends on Mary Beth. I assume she's going to call Matthew to testify."

"What makes you say that?" Phoebe cocked her head and gazed at Luana. Her light-brown eyes had a piercing quality that gave people the impression she could see right through them.

"Because of Greg's testimony yesterday," said Luana. "He said Matthew could back him up about the go-kart being in good condition right before he took it out for the practice run, remember?"

"Oh yeah. But would Mary Beth call him just for that?" asked Phoebe.

"I would. Greg doesn't have any proof Declan caused the accident other than his own opinion," said Luana. "The only thing he's said is the go-kart was working perfectly, so the crash must have been Declan's fault. I admit it makes sense, but it's not exactly proof." She twirled a braid around her finger as she spoke.

"So if we can show there was something wrong with the go-kart, or even that there could have been something wrong with it, that would go a long way to annihilating Greg's argument, and he'd probably lose the case." Luana bit the inside of her cheek to prevent herself from smiling as she watched Phoebe closely.

A frown descended on Phoebe's face. "Annihilate?"

Luana shrugged, feigning indifference. "You know what I mean," she said, trying not to laugh.

"Yes, I do. But that's not the point. Why couldn't you just say destroy like a regular kid?" Phoebe shook her head.

Luana laughed. "Pheebs, you're such a hypocrite! You scold me for using big words, but you always know what they mean. What does that say about you?"

"That's not the point," said Phoebe.

Luana rolled her eyes. "Anyway, as I was saying, if we can prove something could have been wrong with the go-kart, that would go a long way to destroying Greg's argument. So, it benefits him to bring in all the evidence that strengthens his claim the go-kart was in good shape when he gave it to Declan to drive."

"You're right. But what are we going to do to show he's wrong?" asked Declan.

Luana tapped a finger to her cheek. "Well, Greg already admitted you weren't going too fast when you took that last curve before running into the tree, didn't he? If the speed you were traveling had nothing to do with the crash, that just leaves the driving. Greg specifically mentioned the steering when he said you were at fault. He said you wrenched the steering wheel, which caused you to lose control of the go-kart."

"Greg was telling the truth. I did wrench the steering wheel," Declan admitted. "But that's because when I turned it the first time, the go-kart didn't respond. It kept going straight. That's when I straightened out the steering a little, then yanked it."

"Greg said nothing about you turning the steering wheel twice." Luana knitted her brows. "He only said you wrenched it. He might not have noticed you turned the wheel a second time, or he's conveniently not mentioning it. Either way, if we can find anything that shows something amiss with the steering, I think we have a good chance at winning this case." Her frown deepened. "There's something odd about how the steering column broke off the front axle, but I can't figure out what."

"I dunno. It doesn't seem strange to me. Even though I slowed the kart down before the crash, I still hit the tree at a pretty good speed."

"But don't you think it's odd that the only part

of the go-kart that broke was the steering column?" asked Luana. "Greg said he used the same steel for the entire kart, so how come nothing else broke? Apart from a bent front axle and twisted frame, all the rest of the steel is intact."

"You'll figure it out soon enough." Phoebe patted Luana's shoulder. "You always do."

"Thanks for the vote of confidence, Pheebs."

The other court members began trickling in, ending the trio's conference.

"Hi, guys." Ashley strolled to the plaintiff's table and sat down.

"Where's your sister?" Phoebe glanced toward the door, looking for Mary Beth.

"Oh, she'll be along in a minute. She's talking to our next witness."

"Let me guess," said Phoebe. "Matthew Foster?"

"How did you know?" Ashley's blue eyes widened.

"I'm psychic." Phoebe winked.

Luana giggled. "Stop that, Phoebe," she said, seeing Ashley's wide-eyed expression. "We just figured Mary Beth would call Matthew to back up Greg's claim there was nothing wrong with the go-kart right before the crash."

"Oh, I see." Ashley gave them a sheepish smile.

Shortly, Mary Beth, Greg, and Matthew entered the courtroom. Although only ten, Matthew was already almost as tall as his brother.

"Hi, guys." Luana waved to the group.

Matthew gave her a shy smile. "What's up, Luana?"

"Nothing much." She grinned. "How was camp? I see you got a great tan." Matthew had just spent the previous two weeks at a wilderness day camp.

"It was great. I got to do a lot of swimming and canoeing out on the lake." He advanced closer to her and lowered his voice. "Do you know why I'm here?"

Luana studied the younger boy, thinking he seemed tense. *Maybe he's just nervous about testifying.* "Didn't Mary Beth explain why she asked you to come?"

"Um, she said she needed to ask me some questions about Greg's go-kart."

"That's right. I'm guessing she wants you to testify whether there was anything wrong with the kart before Greg took it out for that last practice run."

Matthew's face turned white beneath his tan, and he ran the fingers of both hands through his ash-blond hair. "I—I wouldn't know anything about that. I didn't go out with Greg and Declan the day of the crash."

"Mary Beth knows that. Don't worry." Luana gave his hand a quick squeeze. "You don't need to be nervous. All you have to do is answer the questions as honestly as possible, and if you don't know the answer, just say so. It's no big deal." She glanced down and noticed a green smudge on her hand. "What's that?" she murmured to herself.

"Hmm? What's what?"

"This." She held up her hand so he could see it.

Matthew gave her a rueful smile. "Oh, that. It's paint from my hand. I've been helping Mom create a mural on my little cousin's bedroom wall. It's a present for her fifth birthday. Mom and I have been leaving paint flecks on everything we touch."

He lifted his green-stained hands and showed them to Luana. "See? Mom wants the mural to be 3D, so we're painting cutouts of some parts of the scene that we'll attach to the wall. I was working on the trees this morning." He grimaced. "My hands aren't usually this bad, though. I forgot to wash them when Greg came to get me to come over here for court."

Luana inspected his hands and giggled. "It looks like you're changing into a green alien."

Matthew gave her a weak smile, and Luana noticed he still looked pale.

"Do you want to go wash your hands?" she suggested, thinking he could use the time alone to pull himself together. "You have a few minutes before we get started."

"Yeah, I think I'll do that." Matthew turned and fled the room, with Luana staring after him wonderingly.

CHAPTER 7

A Nervous Wreck

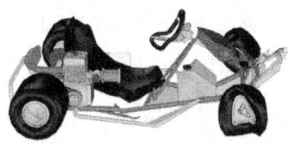

WITHIN MINUTES, ALL the children arrived, Matthew returned to the courtroom, and Heather declared the court in session. "Miss Mary Beth, do you have other witnesses or evidence to present to the court?"

"Yes, Your Honor," said Mary Beth. "I call Matthew Foster to the witness chair."

"Mr. Matthew, come forward, please," said Heather. "Bailiff, you may swear in the witness."

Jake ambled over. "Please raise your right hand. Do you promise to tell the truth, the whole truth, and nothing but the truth?"

Matthew raised his hand. "I do."

"Mr. Matthew, you may sit in the witness chair." Once Matthew sat down, Heather signaled to Mary Beth. "Go ahead."

"Okie, dokie." Mary Beth flipped a page in her

notepad. "Good morning, Mr. Matthew."

"Morning."

"What is your relationship with the plaintiff, Greg Foster?"

"He's my big brother."

"And you know the defendant, Declan Mathias?"

Matthew nodded. "Yes. Declan is Greg's best friend. He's my friend too."

"Your brother, Greg, built a go-kart, didn't he?"

"Yes, he did."

"Did you help him build it?"

"Yeah, I did."

"Did anyone else help?"

"Our dad drew up the plans and helped with some of the building, but Greg did most of the work."

"Anyone else?"

"Declan helped, too."

"OK. Were you there the first time your brother took the go-kart out for a test drive?" asked Mary Beth.

"Yes, I was."

"What did he do before he took the kart out that first time?"

"I'm not sure what you're asking." Matthew puckered his forehead.

THE GO-KARTASTROPHE

"Did he examine it or check it out to make sure it was, you know, working right?"

"Oh. Yes. Yes, Greg and our dad went over it with a fine-tooth comb."

"And did they find anything wrong with it?"

"No, they didn't."

"What about the day of the accident? Did Greg inspect the go-kart that day?"

Matthew squirmed in his seat. "I'm not sure."

"You don't remember your brother inspecting the go-kart on the day the accident happened?"

"Er—no." Matthew swallowed hard and lowered his gaze to his lap.

Watching the boy, Luana frowned.

"Oh, OK then." Mary Beth peeked over her shoulder at Greg to gauge his reaction to his brother's testimony. Greg was staring at Matthew, his mouth set in a hard line. Mary Beth wet her lips and returned her attention to the court. "Your Honor, I have no—"

"You were there when I inspected the kart that day, Matty! Don't you remember?" Greg burst out.

Mary Beth winced as Greg's strident tone pierced her ears.

Heather banged the gavel. "Order in the court! Mr. Greg, you can't just butt in whenever you feel like it. We have a system here."

"Yeah, but what am I supposed to do when a witness remembers wrong?"

Heather's eyes narrowed. "That's why you have an attorney. It's her job to bring out the information that's needed."

"Well, from what I can tell, she's not doing such a good job." Greg sneered.

Mary Beth shot him a frosty look.

"Greg, remember you promised to follow the court's rules?" Heather glared at him, clenching her fist around the gavel as though trying to prevent herself from throwing it at him.

"Yes, I remember," he said through gritted teeth.

"Good. So, can we get on with it?" asked Heather.

"Yeah, yeah. By all means, let's get on with it," Greg said, rolling his eyes.

Heather eyed him balefully before motioning for Mary Beth to continue. The sooner they got this trial over with, the better.

"Er–Mr. Matthew," said Mary Beth, "your brother seems certain you were there when he examined the go-kart the day of the crash. Are you sure you don't remember that?"

Matthew tugged at the neck of his t-shirt. "Um,

now—now that you mention it, I do remember." He forced a smile. "Greg inspected the tires and the brakes."

That's strange, Luana thought, a line creasing her forehead. *Matthew seems almost reluctant to back up Greg's story. I wonder why. Could Greg have lied when he said he inspected the go-kart that day?*

"Did he check anything else?" said Mary Beth.

Matthew shook his head. "Um, no, I—I don't think so."

"Thank you, Mr. Matthew. I have no more questions for this witness, Your Honor."

"Can I go now?" Matthew poised on the edge of the chair, ready to bolt. Sweat beaded his forehead.

"Not so fast." Heather extended an arm in front of Matthew to prevent him from getting up. "I think Miss Luana may have a few questions for you."

He slumped back in the witness chair and ran a hand through his hair. "But Mom's waiting. We're going to Aunt Lucy's to work on Kylie's mural."

"You've got time, Matty," said Greg. "Mom said she wasn't leaving for another thirty minutes."

"Besides, I'm sure Luana will be quick," said Heather. "Won't you, Miss Luana?"

"Yes, Your Honor. I only have a few questions."

Luana strode to the lectern. "Mr. Matthew, you testified your brother inspected the go-kart the first time he took it out for a practice run. Is that correct?"

"Yes."

"How many times did he take the go-kart out?"

"Um, I'm not sure. Greg took it out a lot."

"Were you with him every time he took it for a practice run?"

"No. I went most of the time, but not always. I wasn't there the day of the accident."

"You said your brother inspected the go-kart that day, correct?"

"Yeah."

"He checked the tires and the brakes. Is that right?"

"Um, yes."

"I tested the steering too, Matty! Don't you remember?" Greg exclaimed.

"Order in the court!" Heather pummeled the gavel against her desk. "I'm tired of your outbursts, Greg. For crying out loud, can't you control yourself for five minutes?"

"But he's gonna make me lose the case!" Greg's lips drew back in a snarl, and he fisted both hands on his thighs.

THE GO-KARTASTROPHE

"That's not how it works," said Heather. "You can't just shout out the information you want a witness to give the court. If you think he should know more than he's saying, I suggest you discuss it with your attorney—*quietly*. If she needs to, she can ask your brother more questions after Luana's finished. It's called a re-direct." Heather had spent countless hours researching proper court procedure on the internet ever since she'd taken on the role of the judge in the Kids' Court. "Now be quiet and let Luana finish her cross-examination."

"What about it, Matthew?" said Luana. "Did your brother check the steering? He seems pretty sure he did."

"He did. I guess I just forgot," Matthew said. "It's a little intense testifying. I'm kinda nervous."

"You're doing great. I only have a few more questions." Luana gave him a reassuring smile. "How did Greg check the steering?"

"Excuse me?" Matthew blinked.

"Did he rotate the steering wheel to see if the tires moved in the right direction, or did he examine under the go-kart?"

Matthew's face turned beet red. "He spun the steering wheel a few times and made sure both front tires moved in the right direction."

"Did Declan go on any practice runs when you were there?"

"Yes."

"How many times would you say?"

"I'm not sure. A lot. Declan went with us most times."

"And did Greg allow Declan to drive the go-kart any of those times?"

"Oh, yes. Declan drove the kart lots of times."

"Was he good at driving the go-kart?"

Matthew shrugged. "He handled it well enough and seemed to know what he was doing." He glanced guiltily at his brother. "Greg's a much better driver, though."

"Thank you, Mr. Matthew. Your Honor, I have no further questions for this witness. But I may need to recall him—I mean, I might need him to come back. So could the court instruct Mr. Matthew to remain available in case he's needed again?"

THE GO-KARTASTROPHE

"Er—O . . . K." Heather tilted her head to one side, frowning as she stared at Luana. "Is that allowed?"

Luana grinned. "Yes, it is. Sometimes, lawyers do that if they think they might have more questions for a witness. Daddy says it's good practice to do it routinely. You never know when you might need a witness to come back. Anyhow, you just order him to make himself available if we need him to return to court."

"You mean I'll have to come back?" Matthew's face blanched.

"I doubt it," said Luana. "It's no big deal. Really." She eyed him with concern. Matthew looked like he'd be sick any minute. "There's a good chance I won't need you. Lawyers do it in real life, so the court doesn't lose its subpoena power over a witness."

Matthew's brown eyes widened. "Say what?"

"A subpoena is a court order—written or verbal—instructing a person to come to court on a specific day and time. It does other things too, but that's not important right now. Once a person gets served with a subpoena, the court can have them arrested if they don't show up." Luana frowned. "People don't seem to enjoy coming to court for some reason. I'm not sure why."

"OK, so you won't need me to come back?" Matthew pressed.

"I might, but I doubt it." Luana flashed him a smile.

"OK, then." Matthew's shoulders sagged with relief.

"You can go now, Mr. Matthew, but you must come back if we need you. Do you understand?" Heather gave him a stern look.

"Yeah, sure." Matthew bolted from his chair and hurried from the courtroom without a backward glance.

"Well, Miss Mary Beth, do you have any other witnesses?"

"No, Your Honor," said Mary Beth. "The plaintiff rests."

"You're going to rest?" Greg's eyebrows shot up.

Ashley giggled. "Not that kind of rest, Greg. Mary Beth means we've finished presenting your side of the case. We have no more witnesses or evidence to give to the court."

"Oh. So what happens now?" asked Greg.

"It's the defense's turn." This time it was Mary Beth who answered. "Luana will now call witnesses or give other evidence to the court for Declan."

"Do you have any witnesses to call, Miss Luana?"

said Heather.

"Yes, Your Honor. I intend to call my client. But if the court is agreeable, I'd like to do my direct examination at the crash site."

Heather's eyes riveted to Luana's face. "You want to go to the trails?"

"Yes."

"Oh." Heather considered a moment. "OK. Does that work for everyone?" She scanned the other children's faces and saw they were all in agreement. "All right, then. Make sure you tell your parents where we're going. The trails are a long way from here. We should ride our bikes and take the streets rather than go through the woods." She grimaced. The last time they'd trekked through the woods, her brand-new white sneakers had gotten dirty. "We're going to be gone for a while. How about we each bring a packed lunch and have a picnic after we finish with court?"

"That's a great idea!" Ashley's eyes shone.

"Good, let's meet in front of my house in about ten minutes. That OK?" When everyone agreed, Heather banged the gavel. "Court is in recess."

CHAPTER 8

Trials and Trails

"WHY DIDN'T I know about this place?" Mary Beth regarded the scenery with wide eyes.

The children stood on a grassy knoll overlooking the acclaimed trails. It was a hilly terrain intersected with a long, winding dirt track several feet wide that veered off in various directions.

The trails were on the far side of the conservation land bordering their neighborhood. The journey to get to them was difficult as they had to either walk a couple of miles through dense woods or travel the long way by road. This explained why so few younger kids knew about the area—or, if they did, why they had never been there.

Phoebe wrinkled her nose. "I don't think you've been missing anything. It's just a dirt track."

"That's not true. This place is amazing." Jake

stood with his hands on his hips, eyes bright, lips parted, and admired the landscape.

"Where did the accident happen?" Luana asked Declan.

"Down there." He gestured to an area a little way off, almost directly below where they stood.

Luana put down her bicycle's kickstand, then headed in the direction Declan had pointed, leaving the bike behind. The other children did the same and followed. When they arrived at the crash site, she said, "Which tree did you hit?"

"This one." Declan walked to a nearby tree. "See, here's the groove where the kart took a chunk out of it on impact." He ran his fingers along a gouge where something had slammed into the tree.

Luana moved to stand beside him and peered at

the damage to the tree trunk. At the tree's base was a thick growth of pink wildflowers. She could see where the go-kart had cut a crude path through the flower bed, destroying several plants before smashing into the tree.

"We should get started," said Heather. "You ready, Lindsey?"

"I just need a minute." Lindsey took off the backpack she wore and removed her laptop. Then she sat cross-legged in a nearby grassy area and quickly set up the computer. "I'm ready."

"OK, everyone, the court is now in session." Heather retrieved the gavel from the jeans pocket where she'd stuck it and thumped it against a nearby tree trunk. "Miss Luana, you may begin."

"Thank you, Your Honor. The defense calls Mr. Declan to the . . ." Luana's voice trailed off as she looked around. "I guess there's no witness chair." She gave a wry smile. "I call Mr. Declan to testify."

"Deputy Jake, please swear in the witness," said Heather.

Jake gave the oath, and once Declan promised to tell the truth, Luana began her direct examination. "Mr. Declan, who was driving Greg's go-kart when it crashed?"

"I was."

"Had you driven the go-kart before that day?"

"Yes, lots of times."

"How about before that? Have you ever driven a go-kart before Greg's?"

"Yes. Greg had another go-kart—a wooden one we built together last year. We used to drive it around his yard and the neighborhood. His mom dislikes go-karts, so she was very strict about when and where we could drive it. Aside from that, I've driven the occasional go-kart. You know, at carnivals and stuff."

"Would you say you're familiar with go-karts and how they operate?"

Declan shrugged. "I'm no expert, but I'm a fairly skilled driver. Mr. Foster taught me at the same time as Greg."

"Where were you driving when the accident happened?" asked Luana.

"On this trail." Declan gestured to the makeshift track alongside where they stood.

"Tell us how the crash came about."

"I was coming from that direction." Declan pointed to his right, where the track veered off around a curve and disappeared.

"So you were coming from the north, traveling south?" said Luana. "We need specifics so Lindsey can add them to the record."

"Yes, I was traveling from north to south," said Declan. "Just as I approached the corner, I slowed down some and turned the steering wheel to go around the bend. But the kart kept going straight. I wasn't sure what was going on. I had the steering wheel pulled as far to the right as possible, but nothing. So, I straightened it out a little, then pulled it hard. But the kart still didn't turn, and the next thing I knew, I was heading right for that tree!" He jerked a thumb over his shoulder at the tree behind them.

Declan rolled his shoulders. "I slammed on the brakes, but it was already too late. The kart slowed down, but I knew it would hit the tree, so I bailed. It all happened so fast that parts of it were a blur. It's a good thing I jumped out. Otherwise, I would have gotten hurt."

Greg snorted.

Luana headed in the direction from which Declan said he had been traveling. "So, you were coming from this direction going south?" She raised her voice so Lindsey and the others could hear her as she moved away from the group.

"Yes."

Luana strode further along the track and

disappeared around the curve. A minute later, she came jogging back into view. "You drove around that corner, traveling south in this direction?" She gestured with her hands as she spoke.

"Yes."

"What did you do as you approached the curve?"

"I turned the steering wheel to go around the bend."

"In which direction did you turn the steering wheel?"

"To the right," said Declan. "As you can see, the trail curves to the right. So I had to turn the tires to the right to go around the bend."

"What happened when you spun the steering wheel?"

"Nothing. The go-kart kept going straight. That's when I straightened out the steering wheel, then pulled it to the right a second time."

"What happened then?"

"Nothing. Well, *something* happened." Declan cringed. "I hit the tree."

"As you traveled around the curve, on what side of the trail was the tree you hit?"

"It was on the left. I pulled the steering wheel to the right, but the kart kept going straight, and it ended up hitting a tree on my left."

THE GO-KARTASTROPHE

Luana studied the area. *What could've gone wrong?* "I have no more questions for this witness, Your Honor."

"Very good," said Heather. "Miss Mary Beth, do you have questions for Mr. Declan?"

"I–" Mary Beth shuffled her feet as she stared at Heather. "I'm not sure. I, um . . ." She lifted a shoulder in a vague half-shrug.

Heather sighed. "Do you have any idea when you'll know if you intend to question him? We don't have all day."

Mary Beth swallowed. "I–I have a few questions." She bit her lip.

"Well, what are you waiting for?" said Heather. "Go ahead."

Mary Beth winced. "Mr. Declan, you say you turned the steering wheel to the right?"

"Yes, I did."

"But the tree you hit was on your left, wasn't it?"

"Yes."

"How do you explain that?"

"It's simple," said Declan. "The tires didn't turn when I spun the steering wheel. They should have turned to the right. I would have gone around the bend with no problem if they had. It's like I've been saying all along–something was wrong with the go-kart's steering."

"Er—yes, yes, you said that." Mary Beth's ears turned red.

Phoebe snickered.

Luana nudged her in the arm. "Be nice, Pheebs."

"But don't you see? Mary Beth is proving our point—there was something wrong with the go-kart," Phoebe whispered.

"I know. But this is Mary Beth's first time cross-examining a witness, and it's not as easy as it looks."

"Do you have to be so nice all the time?" Phoebe huffed.

Luana grinned. "You wouldn't want me any other way."

Phoebe rolled her eyes but smiled, knowing Luana was right. She went back to listening to Mary Beth's cross-examination of Declan.

"But we only have your word for it that there was something wrong with the go-kart, right?" Mary Beth was saying to Declan.

He shrugged. "I'm not sure what you expect me to say to that."

"Isn't it true you drove around the curve too fast?"

"No, that is *not* true. I was going about twenty,

maybe twenty-five miles per hour. Greg's gone around this bend way faster than that! He said so himself just yesterday when he testified."

"Er—y-yes. Yes, he did. But isn't it true you don't have my client's experience driving go-karts?"

"No, that isn't true, either. It's like I said before. Greg had another kart before this one. We both used to drive it around. And I've driven other go-karts," said Declan. "I will admit he's the better driver, though."

"Obviously." Mary Beth sniffed, sticking her nose in the air. "Since you're the one who crashed the go-kart."

"That wasn't my fault!" Declan clenched his fists at his sides. "The accident could've happened to anyone driving the kart."

"So you say. But the fact is, my client drove the go-kart around this same track several times with no problems before he allowed you to drive it. Isn't that right?"

"Yeah, I guess."

"Well, then." Mary Beth gave him a self-satisfied smile. "I have no further questions for this witness."

"Now I ask you, Lu, what was the point of that cross-examination?" said Phoebe.

Luana covered her mouth, hiding a smile behind her hand, and shrugged. Mary Beth had achieved nothing with her cross-examination of Declan—nothing except to emphasize he'd pulled the steering wheel to the right yet had hit a tree on his left. A fact that did not help Greg.

Heather declared the court in recess, and the group returned to their bikes.

"Oh, goodie," said Jake. "Time to eat. I'm starving!"

Ashley giggled. Jake was always hungry!

That afternoon, Luana, Phoebe, and Declan sat in the courtroom discussing their next move. Luana sat cross-legged on the floor by the go-kart, which lay on its side. Jake, who oversaw all the evidence, had written the letter "A" on a sticky note and attached it to one of the kart's sides. As Luana sat staring at the vehicle, Phoebe and Declan discussed the events in court earlier that day.

"What was Mary Beth's deal?" said Declan. "She acted like she'd won an award when she got done questioning me."

Phoebe laughed. "That's Mary Beth for you. Half the time, she has no idea what she's doing, yet she's convinced she's a legal guru. All because she spends hours watching cheesy courtroom dramas on television."

"Well, she certainly made a fool of herself today. I couldn't believe she asked me how I'd ended up hitting the tree on my left if I'd turned the steering wheel to the right." Declan chuckled. "Doesn't that prove my point there was something wrong with the kart?"

"It sure does." Phoebe nodded, her silky black hair swaying around her head. "Besides, Greg had already testified he saw you pull the steering wheel to the right. If you did, and the kart continued straight, that proves something was wrong with it." Golden flecks glowed in her brown eyes. "I think we're going to win your case, Declan!" She hugged herself. "Don't you think so, Luana?"

When Luana didn't reply, Phoebe glanced over her shoulder at her friend. Luana stared unseeing at the go-kart, a faraway expression on her face as she tugged mercilessly on a braid.

Sighing, Phoebe got up, walked over to Luana, and gently removed the hair from her fingers.

Luana jolted and raised her eyes to Phoebe. "Did you say something, Pheebs?"

"You're sabotaging your braid."

"Sabotaging?" Luana's brow creased.

"Yes, sabotaging. You're not the only one who can use big words, you know. What would you call it? You're deliberately destroying the braid." She pointed to Luana's hair.

Luana's frown deepened as she gazed at the braid she'd been tugging. Almost half of it had unraveled. She grimaced and began to re-braid the hair. "OK, so I messed up a braid. But to say I sabotaged it seems a bit–" Luana dropped her hair and shifted to her knees. Leaning close to the go-kart, she studied its undercarriage.

"What is it, Luana?" Phoebe stared wide-eyed at her friend, sensing Luana's excitement.

"Sabotage!" Luana lifted sparkling eyes to Phoebe. "Pheebs, you're a genius! I think I know what caused the accident!"

"You do?" Phoebe's mouth fell open.

"Yes!" Luana jumped to her feet and darted toward the door. "Come on, you two! We've got work to do!"

CHAPTER 9

Dance of Truth

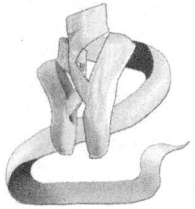

"MISS LUANA, ARE you ready to begin?" asked Heather.

"I am, Your Honor."

"Very good. You may call your next witness."

"I call Matthew Foster to the witness chair."

Matthew stepped forward from the back of the courtroom. His skin was sickly pale beneath his tan, and dark circles stood out under his brown eyes. When he sat down, Heather reminded him he was still under oath.

Matthew gave a jerky nod and began running his hands through his hair, as was his habit.

Luana studied his appearance. *Poor kid. He looks terrified. I wonder if he got any sleep last night?* Matthew had sounded panicked on the phone when she'd called the night before to tell him she needed him to return to court. "Hi, Matthew," she said gently.

"Hi." His voice was strained, barely above a whisper.

"You seem nervous. Try to relax, OK? I only have a few questions for you. Everything's going to be all right. I promise." Luana gave him her warmest smile, hoping to reassure him.

"OK." Matthew nodded, but his posture remained stiff and upright.

"You love your big brother, Greg, don't you?"

"Yes, of course I do."

"One could even say you idolize him. Isn't that right?"

Matthew gave a half-shrug. "I guess. Greg's an awesome big brother."

"How did you feel about him entering the Tri-County Race-A-Thon?" Luana cocked her head and stared at Matthew as he answered her question, her eyes taking in every detail of his appearance.

"I was excited for him. I knew how much he wanted to race. Ever since he was a little kid, Greg has dreamed of following in Dad's footsteps and winning a division trophy."

"But your mom had doubts about him entering the race, didn't she?"

"Yeah, Mom doesn't like go-karts at all. Greg

THE GO-KARTASTROPHE

would never have even driven one if it were up to her. She says they're too dangerous and only let him have a kart last year because Dad convinced her he could teach Greg to be a safe driver. She still thought they were dangerous, though."

"If your mom thought go-kart racing was so dangerous, do you know why she changed her mind about your brother entering the race?" asked Luana.

"She didn't change her mind—not really. I think Dad and Greg wore her down. That and she knows Greg is an excellent driver. He's a natural, just like our dad. But she was still worried even though she agreed to let him race." Matthew gripped his hands together so tight his knuckles turned white. "Greg had to promise to be extra careful before she gave in. And even then, I know she didn't want him to do it." He gave a weary sigh.

"How do you know that?" asked Luana.

"Oh, things she'd say from time to time. And a few nights before the accident, I overheard her and Dad talking about the Race-A-Thon. She said she'd read a news article about a girl getting scalped in a go-kart accident. The girl's hair got caught in the engine and ripped out, causing injuries to her head." Matthew shuddered. "Mom said she'd never even thought of that possibility. The accident made her realize go-karting was way more dangerous than she'd thought. Mom wanted to tell Greg she'd changed her mind about letting him race, but Dad told her she couldn't do that. He said if she did, Greg and I would get the idea it was OK to go back on promises."

"So, your mom wanted to stop Greg from racing, but your dad wouldn't let her back out of the agreement?"

"Yes."

"Your mom is painting a mural for your cousin's birthday, isn't she?"

Matthew's eyes darted to Luana, a slight frown on his face. "Um, yes. She is."

"And you're helping her with it, aren't you?"

"Yes, I am." Matthew relaxed his stiff posture a little. "We're painting it for Kylie's fifth birthday. She's big into ballet right now, so Mom decided on a scene with ballerinas dancing in a forest." A corner of his mouth quirked up. "Kylie's such a baby, but she's totally adorable."

"I see your hands are yellow today." Luana smiled as she inclined her chin toward his hands.

Matthew glanced down. "Er—yes. I was painting sunflowers this morning."

THE GO-KARTASTROPHE

"I suppose you've been leaving specks of yellow paint all over the place, huh?" She grinned.

"Yeah, you could say that." Matthew forced a smile.

"What about your mom?" asked Luana.

"What about her?"

"Has she been leaving paint smudges on things, too?"

"Yes, she has," said Matthew. "I think I told you that yesterday."

"Have you, by any chance, used any pink paint in this mural?"

"Yes, of course. Can you paint a mural for a five-year-old girl and not use pink? It's Kylie's favorite color, so there's a lot of pink in the mural."

"When did you use the pink paint?"

"Um, I'm not sure. Is it important?" Matthew again ran a hand through his hair.

"Think about it," said Luana. "Try to remember."

"Well, we started the mural, not this past weekend, but the weekend before. Then Mom worked Monday and Tuesday. She works twelve-hour shifts, so that's pretty much all she does on the days she goes to the hospital. Anyhow, we started the mural on Saturday, painted a little on Sunday, and didn't get back to it until Wednesday."

"So, last Wednesday?" asked Luana. "Is that when you used the pink paint?"

"Yeah." Matthew nodded. "Wednesday, Thursday. That's when we started painting the dancers. A couple of them are wearing pink tutus."

"Who used the pink paint, you or your mother?"

"Both of us."

"How—"

"What's with all the questions about murals and paint?" Greg demanded.

"Please be quiet, Mr. Greg, and let Miss Luana finish her questions." Heather's eyes narrowed as she glared at Greg. "Although, I'm curious too, Luana."

"It will all become clear in just a little while," said Luana. *At least, I hope so.* "How did it make you feel when you overheard your mother talking about the girl injured in the go-kart accident?" she asked Matthew, switching the focus of her questions.

He shrugged. "I dunno. Nervous, I guess."

"Nervous?" Luana raised her eyebrows. "Why nervous?"

"Because Mom was worried about the potential danger, but Dad wouldn't let her stop Greg from racing. It scared me."

THE GO-KARTASTROPHE

"You were scared," she said. "Were you scared enough to stop Greg from entering the race yourself?"

Matthew licked his lips and rubbed his palms back and forth on his denim shorts. "I–I–I don't know what you mean."

"Did you do anything to stop your brother from entering the race?" Luana's voice was gentle but firm, and she held Matthew's eyes with her own, noticing how his pupils flared as she asked the question.

Matthew swallowed hard, tugging at the collar of his t-shirt as if it were suddenly too tight for him. Beads of sweat appeared on his upper lip.

"What the–" Greg shot up from his chair. "What's going on, Luana? You know Declan's guilty, so in a desperate attempt to save him, you're accusing my *brother*?"

"Mr. Greg. Sit. Down." Heather's nostrils flared. Greg ignored her and remained standing, his blazing eyes fixed on Luana, shooting daggers at her.

Luana kept her focus on Matthew. "Matthew?" Her voice was soft and coaxing. He had yet to answer her question.

"Answer her, Matty," said Greg. "Tell her you did

nothing."

Heather frowned at Greg with her mouth set in a hard line.

Matthew stared at Luana, stone-faced. He said nothing.

"That's it," said Greg after the silence had stretched on for a while. "We're done here. If this is how you conduct a trial, I want no part of it. Come on, Matty, we're leaving." He stomped toward the door.

"No, Greg." Matthew squared his shoulders as he spoke, his voice strained. "Don't leave. Luana's right. I did something to the go-kart."

Loud gasps echoed throughout the courtroom as the children reacted to his announcement. *Had Matthew just confessed to deliberately tampering with Greg's go-kart?*

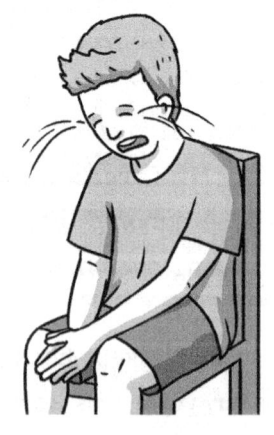

Greg's jaw dropped. "What—what are you saying, Matty?" he said when he finally found his voice. "What did you do to my kart?" His voice rose.

Matthew shook his head. He opened his mouth

to speak, but no words came. Then, lowering his head, he sobbed loud, heart-wrenching sobs that shook his entire body.

Luana ran to him and put her arms around his shoulders. "Can't you see your brother's upset, Greg? Don't yell at him!"

"*He's* upset?" Greg gave a bitter laugh. "What about me? It's *my* go-kart that got wrecked! Not to mention I've been fighting with my best friend for days. And now you tell me my *brother* stabbed me in the back?"

Luana ignored Greg's outburst and continued to comfort Matthew. "I'll tell them what I know, and you can fill in the rest when you're ready. OK?" she whispered to the troubled boy.

Matthew nodded, still sobbing, though quieter now.

"Matthew tampered with your go-kart, Greg," she said, raising her voice so they could all hear her. "But he did it with the best of intentions."

"Oh, I see. Well, that makes it all OK then." Greg's voice was heavy with sarcasm.

"He did it because he was afraid you'd get hurt. He did it for you."

"Ooh, it's another Perry Mason moment!" Mary Beth bounced in her seat; her blue eyes gleamed.

"Who?" asked Declan.

"Some old guy who was a television lawyer," said Phoebe. "Mary Beth is obsessed with courtroom shows."

"Perry Mason is not 'some old guy,'" Mary Beth protested. "He was an amazing lawyer, and in every episode, there was a moment in court when he'd reveal the bad guy's identity. He was brilliant!"

"Stop your yammering, Mary Beth," said Greg. "I want to hear what Luana has to say."

"Oh, sorry." Mary Beth's face turned red. "Go ahead, Luana."

"Thanks, Mary Beth." Luana scanned the faces of her friends, all of whom were staring at her with rapt attention. Her lips curved into a slight smile. "I know what caused the go-kart accident."

CHAPTER 10

All's Well That Ends Well

LUANA'S SMILE WIDENED as she observed her friends' shocked faces. "Mrs. Foster worried about Greg entering the go-kart race. Everyone knows go-karts can be dangerous. But Mrs. Foster is a nurse, so she knows better than most people how dangerous they can be. Despite her fears, however, she agreed to let Greg race. But when she heard about that latest go-kart accident, she had second thoughts."

"Do you mean the scalping accident?" Jake scratched at his temple. For once, he was paying attention. Usually, he sat in his chair daydreaming, only half aware of the goings-on in court.

"Exactly, Jake," said Luana. "Matthew got scared when he overheard his parents talking about it. Especially when he realized his mom didn't want

Greg to race anymore, but his dad wouldn't let her go back on her agreement to allow him to enter the Race-A-Thon. Matthew decided if his parents wouldn't stop Greg from racing, he would have to stop Greg himself. But talking to Greg was out of the question. Matthew knows Greg can be a bit-er–" She gestured vaguely with one hand, searching for the right word.

"Pigheaded?" Phoebe smirked at Greg.

He glared back at her, then returned his attention to Luana.

Luana chuckled. "I was going to say determined. The point is Matthew knew talking to Greg wouldn't make a difference. Greg was going to enter the race, and that was that. Matthew had to stop his brother from racing, so he decided to make the go-kart inoperable somehow. That way, Greg couldn't enter the race."

"But what made you think there was something wrong with the go-kart before the accident?" Lindsey's forehead puckered. Until now, she had been busy typing every word said in court.

"I first realized something was wrong when we examined the go-kart. Phoebe noticed that the edge where the steering column had snapped off from the front axle was partly smooth and jagged.

THE GO-KARTASTROPHE

That seemed odd, but I couldn't think why." Luana pursed her lips. "I also couldn't understand why only the steering column broke during the accident, even though Greg used the same steel to build the entire go-kart. Even the frame, which had absorbed most of the force during the impact, was still in one piece."

"Part jagged, part smooth," said Jake. "That does seem strange, but how'd you figure out someone had tampered with the kart?"

"I didn't think that at first, Jake," said Luana. "It wasn't until yesterday when Phoebe used the word 'sabotage' that it hit me. Sabotage! That was it! If someone had tampered with the go-kart—for example, if they had cut partway through the steering column's steel—that would account for the partially smooth edge where it had separated from the front axle. The jagged part occurred when the rest of the steering column snapped off during the crash."

Jake nodded sagely. "Yep, that makes sense. It's like cutting halfway through a roll, then ripping off the other half." He glanced at Greg's brother, who had stopped crying and now sat quietly with his head down. "But why'd you think it was Matthew?"

"Well, I wondered who would damage Greg's go-kart. And why?" said Luana. "The list of suspects was short. Few people had access to the go-kart. There's Greg, of course, Matthew, and their parents. Declan also had access. I suppose there were other suspects, but these were the most likely ones. They were regularly at the Foster house and had easy access to the go-kart."

"Yes, yes, Luana," said Ashley impatiently. "But what made you think it was Matthew?"

"By process of elimination, Ashley." Luana grinned. "I had to wonder which of them would do such a thing. I couldn't imagine Mr. or Mrs. Foster damaging the kart. Either could have easily put their foot down and told Greg he couldn't race. Not to mention, neither of them would risk hurting the boys by vandalizing the go-kart. I knew it wasn't Declan, of course. He wouldn't damage the go-kart, then drive it, knowing it could fall apart at any minute. So, that just left Matthew."

Jake whistled. "Impressive."

"But there was a problem. I know how much Matthew loves and looks up to his brother, so it didn't make sense that he would try to ruin Greg's chance at doing something he's wanted to do for so long. I also couldn't believe Matthew would want to hurt Greg. But then, I remembered the green paint

THE GO-KARTASTROPHE

on my hand." Luana held up her now clean hands.

"What green paint?" Lindsey had closed her laptop and was sitting with her upper body sprawled on her table, head propped with her right cheek in her hand.

"After I touched Matthew's hand yesterday, I noticed green paint on my palm. He told me about the mural he and Mrs. Foster have been painting for Kylie. Matthew said they've been leaving paint flecks on everything they touch. That's when I realized the pink mark on the go-kart frame was likely paint. Remember, I asked you about it, Greg?"

Luana moved from behind the lectern and walked to the go-kart, still lying on its side in the court's well. She stooped down and pointed to the pink spot on the vehicle's undercarriage. "See that pink mark? It's paint." Scuffling sounds emitted through the courtroom as the other children advanced to get a closer look at the go-kart.

"When Matthew admitted they'd used pink paint on the mural last Wednesday and Thursday, I was certain I was right. I think Matthew damaged the go-kart so that it would fail when Greg took it in for the Race-A-Thon inspection. Once that happened, Greg would be out of the race. I'm just not sure why he did it so soon. There was still almost a week left before the entry process began." She turned to Matthew, a question in her eyes.

Matthew, who had by now fully composed himself, nodded. "You're right, Luana." He looked at his brother. "I'm sorry, Greg. I was terrified when I heard Mom and Dad talking about that girl getting scalped in the go-kart accident. I just had to do something! I knew I couldn't ask you not to race. There's no way you would have agreed to do that. And I figured you'd probably think I was a baby for being so worried." He ran a hand over his face.

"I didn't plan on messing with the kart, though. I swear! I was in the garage looking for some paint remover when I saw the go-kart, and the idea just popped into my head. I didn't stop to think. If I had, I would have waited until closer to the entry period—or maybe I wouldn't have done it at all. I only meant to put a slight cut in the column." He lowered his gaze to his lap.

"A small enough cut, so you wouldn't know anything was wrong, but big enough that the committee would find it during the inspection. I was so sick when I heard about the accident. Declan could've been hurt, and it would have been all my fault! I didn't know what to do. I couldn't fess up because I knew I'd be in big trouble, and I didn't want you to hate me." He raised his head and looked miserably at his brother. Tears rolled down his cheeks.

"But Matty, you know Mom. Do you think Dad could stop her if she really wanted to keep me from entering the race?" Greg ran a hand over his face.

"No, you're right. No matter what Dad said, she would have stood her ground." Matthew covered his face with his hands. "I'm such an idiot."

"You're not an idiot." Greg sighed. "You're a good kid who idolizes his big brother." He grinned. "You can't deny it, you know. It's in the court record. Isn't that right, Lindsey?"

Lindsey's head snapped up, and her breath caught in her throat. "Er—y-yes, th—that's right."

"Let this be a lesson to you, Matthew. The ends don't always justify the means," said Heather.

"What's that mean?" Mary Beth wrinkled her forehead.

"It means, big sister," said Ashley, "that doing something wrong for a good reason doesn't make it right. Matthew tampered with Greg's go-kart because he wanted to keep Greg safe, but tampering with the go-kart was still wrong."

"True," said Luana. "It caused an accident and could have hurt someone. Which, ironically, is the very thing Matthew was trying to prevent."

"You're all right." Matthew gazed at his brother, a pleading look in his eyes. "Can you ever forgive me, Greg?"

Greg sighed again. "Yeah, I forgive you, little brother. How can I not? You did something stupid, but you did it to help me. Besides, this is all my fault."

"How do you figure that?" Matthew frowned.

"If I were a better big brother, you wouldn't have been so scared to come and talk to me. I know I can be pigheaded." Phoebe snorted, but Greg ignored her. "But I promise I will listen to you and consider your feelings from now on. OK?" He gave his brother a light punch in the shoulder.

"OK." Matthew smiled. "And hey, Dec., what can I say? I'm so sorry for everything. Greg blamed you for something I did, and I almost got you hurt. I thought it would blow over, and the two of you would be back on good terms in no time. Honest. I promise I'll make it up to you somehow."

"Don't sweat it, kiddo." Declan waved off his apology. "I wish you'd fessed up on your own, but I get it. It's difficult owning up when you've done something wrong. But there's no harm done." He glanced at the go-kart and grimaced. "Well, except

THE GO-KARTASTROPHE

for the kart. Greg, do you think we can fix it in time to enter the race?"

Greg shrugged. "There's always next year—*if* Mom will let me enter. I'm just mad I lost sight of what's important. I almost ruined our friendship over this." He gave his friend a sheepish look. "What can I say, Dec? I'm an idiot. I'm sorry I was such a jerk about the whole thing."

"Hey, I'm your best friend, aren't I? Let's just put this behind us. But next time I tell you something's wrong, perhaps you could give me the benefit of the doubt?"

"You got it, man." Greg held out his hand to Declan, and the two boys did a fist pump.

"Matty, you know we'll have to tell Mom and Dad what you did, don't you?"

Matthew groaned. "Mom's going to go ballistic! I deserve it, though."

"Don't worry, little brother. I'll stick by you."

"You'd do that, even after all the trouble I've caused?" Matthew gave a slight shake of his head.

"Of course. What are big brothers for?"

"Aw, isn't that sweet? The big, bad jock has a heart, after all." Phoebe smirked at Greg.

He leered back at her.

"OK, everyone." Heather rapped the gavel to get their attention. "I think that's it. Let's sit down so we can finish this."

Everyone returned to their seats, and Matthew sat in the gallery.

"I'm ready to rule in this case—although I doubt it's necessary. After considering all the evidence, I declare Declan Mathias is not guilty. My recommendation is for Mr. Matthew to pay Mr. Greg for his damages. I can't enforce that ruling, of course, seeing as Mr. Matthew is not a party to this case, but . . ." She gave Matthew a meaningful look and raised her eyebrows.

"I understand, Your Honor. And I intend to pay to fix the go-kart." Matthew smiled grimly. "Even if I didn't, I'm sure my parents would make me."

"OK then, that's it, everybody!" Heather banged the gavel. "The Kids' Court is adjourned."

❖ ❖ ❖

Later that afternoon, Luana and Phoebe were lying by the Porcellos' pool.

THE GO-KARTASTROPHE

"This is nice." Phoebe sighed. "Peace at last." A shadow fell across her, blocking out the sun. She opened her eyes and saw Greg standing over her. "What do *you* want?"

"Hey there, Little Bit." He smirked. "I came to say thanks."

"Really?" She raised her eyebrows.

"Yes, really. If it hadn't been for you guys, I would have ruined my friendship with Declan—that or the guilt would have eventually driven Matty crazy. Perhaps both. Anyway, I appreciate what you did. You're not so bad for a couple of little kids."

Phoebe scowled. "I told you to stop calling us that."

Luana laughed. "Don't you get it, Phoebe? Greg does it on purpose because he knows that's the way to get to you."

Phoebe eyed Greg. "Is that true?"

He grinned and winked at her. "I'll never tell." He turned and headed back to his yard. "Thanks a lot, Luana. I owe you one—big time!" He glanced at them over his shoulder as he spoke.

You're welcome.

"You're welcome." Luana flashed him a smile, her dimples on full display. "By the way, what happened with Matthew and your parents?"

Greg pivoted to face them and continued moving backward. "He's grounded until he's eighty, but he'll survive." He rounded a corner and disappeared.

Luana sighed. "As much as I enjoy going to court, it's nice to have some downtime."

"Yup!" Phoebe flipped over onto her stomach. "I'm going to enjoy it while I can because I have a feeling you'll be finding us another case before I know it." She turned her face away from Luana and closed her eyes.

Luana giggled to herself. Phoebe was so right!

If you enjoyed my story, please leave a review giving it two thumbs up! Scan the QR code to go directly to the review page.

Do you want to find out what's next for Luana and Phoebe? Continue reading for a sneak peek at book

THE GO-KARTASTROPHE

#3, *The Goody Bag Goner,* or scan the QR code and order your copy today!

If you haven't already read *The Doll Dilemma*, order a copy and find out how the Kid's Court started. Scan the QR code to go directly to the sales page.

A KIDS' COURT WHODUNIT
THE GOODY BAG GONER
BY CARON PESCATORE

CHAPTER 1

Trick... or Cheat?

"GIVE ME BACK my goody bag!"

"I told you—*I don't have it!*"

"What's going on over there?" Luana Porcello and her best pal, Phoebe Chen, were in the middle of saying goodbye after attending their friend's eleventh birthday party when the loud shouts from the other side of the yard drew their attention.

"Geez, I dunno," said Gigi Hašani. "It sounds like a fight." She twisted a lock of blond hair around her finger and stared across the backyard, where a small group of girls gathered. "I guess I should go find out what's happening." She bit her lip while staring across the yard, not moving.

"We'll go with you, Gigi," said Luana.

Gigi gave her a grateful smile, then started

across the lawn, weaving among the teal and coral decorated tables and chairs her mother had set up for the party. Luana and Phoebe quickly followed.

When they arrived at the scene of the commotion, they discovered two girls in a heated argument.

"Why am I not surprised Kelly is in the middle of this?" Phoebe whispered to Luana. "Trouble seems to follow that girl the way bees follow honey."

Luana smothered a laugh with her hand. "Bees *make* honey, Pheebs. They don't follow it."

Phoebe rolled her eyes. "You know what I meant."

"Yes, but as usual, I had to decipher what you were trying to say."

Phoebe snorted. "Decipher? Do you always have to use such big words? Couldn't you have said figure out like a regular kid?"

Luana batted her long lashes at Phoebe. The dimples in her cheeks deepened as she curved her lips into a mischievous smile. "You love me just the way I am, Pheebs," she said, then nudged her friend in the arm with an elbow. "Now, be quiet so we can listen to what all the fuss is about."

"Rachel probably just took your goody bag to keep it safe, Kelly," said Mary Beth Stover in her usual vague manner.

Phoebe gaped at her, wondering how she could be so clueless. Mary Beth's eyes were so wide-set they made one think of a deer in headlights, and Phoebe thought it was the perfect description for the scatterbrained girl.

"But I *didn't* take it!" said Rachel.

Luana felt a twinge of discomfort in her chest. *Poor Rachel. Kelly must be wrong. Rachel wouldn't take her goody bag—would she?* Luana didn't know Rachel very well; they'd just met that afternoon at the party, as Rachel had only moved into the neighborhood a few days earlier. But the peacemaker in Luana couldn't stand to see anyone unhappy—even a stranger—and she had liked Rachel on sight. "What happened?" she asked, her amber eyes solemn.

"Kelly can't find her goody bag," said Mary Beth.

Phoebe rolled her eyes. "We gathered that much, Mary Beth. What Luana wants to know is what happened—exactly."

"Oh." Mary Beth blinked. "Um, I'm not sure."

Phoebe shook her head. *Figures.*

"*I'll* tell you what happened," Kelly cried. "Rachel stole my goody bag! I left it on that table over there"—she gestured to a table a few feet away—"and it was gone when I returned from using the bathroom! *She* took it." She jabbed a finger in Rachel's direction.

"I did not!" said Rachel.

"Why do you think Rachel took the goody bag, Kelly?" asked Luana.

"I don't *think* she took it. I *know* she did," said Kelly. "We're wasting time. We should search her." She took a step toward Rachel, intent on doing a pat-down search as she'd seen on TV crime shows.

"Hold on, Kelly." Phoebe moved quickly, cutting off Kelly's advancement toward Rachel. "Let's all take a deep breath and calm down."

"Phoebe's right," said Luana. "We need to go about this in an orderly fashion. Rachel, I hate to ask, but did you take Kelly's goody bag?"

"No, I didn't," said Rachel, her voice strained. "You can search me if you like."

Luana glanced at Gigi, who stood wringing her hands. *Poor Gigi. What a way for her birthday party to end*, she thought. Then she sighed, wondering what she should do. She caught Gigi's eyes and raised her eyebrows, silently asking her friend for guidance. Gigi shrugged as if to say, *do whatever you think is best* in response to Luana's unspoken question.

Luana bit off another sigh. "If you're certain you

THE GO-KARTASTROPHE

don't mind, Rachel, would you empty your pockets for us?"

"Gladly." Rachel emptied the pockets of her navy-blue shorts. Among the various items was a teal-colored goody bag.

"That's it!" Kelly exclaimed. "That's my goody bag."

Did Rachel take Kelly's goody bag? To find out, scan the QR code and get your copy of *The Goody Bag Goner* today!

THE LOST LOCKET
A Phoebe Chen Mystery

Eight-year-old Phoebe Chen has her first case to crack. Can you help?

Phoebe loves figuring things out—deciphering puzzles, unscrambling word games, and anything that involves brainstorming. Her fondest wish is to solve mysteries like Nancy Drew—or her police detective father. So when a friend raises the alarm over a missing necklace, Phoebe jumps at the chance to follow in her idol's footsteps and offers to take on the case.

Enlisting the aid of her BFF, Luana, Phoebe gets to work searching for clues, interviewing witnesses, and compiling a list of suspects. But when the evidence seems to implicate a friend, Phoebe realizes being a junior detective isn't all fun and games. Phoebe must find concrete evidence before she points the finger. Can she do it, or will the miscreant get away with their dastardly plot?

 Subscribe to Caron Pescatore's newsletter and get your free copy of *The Lost Locket*. Just scan the QR code.

AUTHOR'S NOTE

Thank you so much for reading *The Go-KartAstrophe*! I hope you had as much fun reading Greg and Declan's story as I had writing it. Greg and Phoebe's constant bickering had me laughing through most of the story. 😂 😂 Phoebe is quite a girl; I admit she's my favorite character. Who's yours, I wonder? 🤭 🤭

If you enjoyed the story, please consider leaving a review on Amazon or your favorite online bookstore, Goodreads, BookBub, and any other online book review website you may frequent. Reviews are a great way to help other readers discover new books!

Do you have a cool idea for a character's name or a case for the Kids' Court? I would love to hear it! Email me at caronpescatore@gmail.com. But check with Mom or Dad first to make sure it's OK!

Sign up for my newsletter to ensure you don't miss out on upcoming releases, book sales, or other news. Scan the QR code on the previous page to subscribe and get your free copy of *The Lost Locket*. I adore hearing from my readers, so please connect with me, @CaronPescatore, on Facebook, Twitter, TikTok, or Instagram.

ABOUT THE AUTHOR

CARON PESCATORE was born in the United Kingdom. She spent her childhood in Jamaica before migrating to the United States. After practicing as a registered nurse for several years, she entered law school, getting her J.D. in 2001. She worked as an attorney for years before leaving the profession to become a stay-at-home mom—her most challenging career to date. Ms. Pescatore is passionate about justice and fairness for all, a sentiment that led, in part, to her decision to write the Kids' Court Whodunit series. Her favorite pastimes are reading, writing, and watching true-crime shows. At present, Ms. Pescatore lives in Florida with her husband and children.

Glossary

Adjourn: To take a break

Attorney: A person licensed to practice law; give legal advice; and speak on behalf of people in court

Bailiff: An officer assigned to a court who keeps order in the courtroom and protects the judge

Bench trial: A trial where the judge decides the outcome of the case instead of a jury

Court reporter: A type of secretary who works in a court and keeps a record of everything said by typing it down

Cross-examination: Formal questioning of a witness by the lawyer who did not call the witness to court

Damages: A sum of money awarded to a person to make up for a loss or injury

Defendant: A person accused of wrongdoing in a court of law

Direct examination: Questioning of a witness by the lawyer who called the witness to court

Evidence: Facts and information that help the court figure out the truth of what happened in a particular case

Gallery: The area in the courtroom where visitors to the court can sit and observe the proceedings

Judge: A public official who decides cases in a court of law

Jury: A group of people who listen to the evidence presented in a trial and determine the outcome

Plaintiff: A person who brings a claim against another in a court of law

A Preponderance of the evidence: The amount of proof the plaintiff must bring to court to convince the judge or jury that the defendant is guilty

Prosecutor: A lawyer who represents the government in a criminal trial

Recall a witness: Calling a witness who has already given testimony to give additional testimony to the court

Redirect: When a lawyer asks his own witness more questions after the other lawyer cross-examines the witness

Rest: A party rests when he finishes presenting evidence to the court

Subpoena: A court order–written or verbal–directing a person to come to court on a specific day and time.

Testify: To give evidence as a witness in court

Testimony: A formal statement made in a court

Trial: A court procedure where facts are presented to a judge or jury to decide the defendant's innocence or guilt.

Well: The space between the judge's bench and counsel tables

Witness: A person who provides evidence in court

Verdict: The outcome in a case deciding who wins and who loses

Made in the USA
Columbia, SC
04 November 2022